NASH
&
ZULLO'S

BELIEVE IT OR ELSE!!

BASEBALL EDITION

Also by Bruce Nash and Allan Zullo:

THE FISHING HALL OF SHAME™

NASH & ZULLO'S

BELIEVE IT OR ELSE!!

BASEBALL EDITION

BRUCE NASH and ALLAN ZULLO

Ray Villwock, *Curator*

A DELL TRADE PAPERBACK

A DELL TRADE PAPERBACK

Published by
Dell Publishing
a division of
Bantam Doubleday Dell Publishing Group, Inc.
666 Fifth Avenue
New York, New York 10103

ISBN: 0-440-50375-2

Layout and text design by Mel Barry

Printed in the United States of America

Published simultaneously in Canada

April 1992

10 9 8 7 6 5 4 3 2 1
RRH

DEDICATION

To my friend Rasha Drachkovitch, for helping me fulfill a childhood dream by producing the TV series "Nash & Zullo's Offbeat Sports Beat."

—Bruce Nash

To Suzanne Williams, a rare and special friend who not only sees good in others, but does good for others.

—Allan Zullo

To Tyson, Whit, and Lexi, my reasons to believe.

—Ray Villwock

ACKNOWLEDGMENTS

We wish to thank those players, coaches, and umpires who shared their amazing stories with us.

This book couldn't have been completed without the assistance and cooperation of the National Baseball Hall of Fame Library in Cooperstown, New York. We especially appreciate the help, guidance, and friendship of senior research associate Bill Deane. We are also grateful for the invaluable research provided by J. Mark Sweeney of the Library of Congress in Washington, D.C., and for the excellent layout and design work of Mel Barry.

For their assistance, we wish to thank Paul Adomites; Jim Barbagallo; David Cohen; Morris Eckhouse, executive director of the Society for American Baseball Research (SABR); Paul Haas, Sports Books, etc.; Bee Hanks, Phenom Sports; Tot Holmes, Holmes Publishing; Tom Macsinka; Bobby Plapinger, Baseball Books; and Guy Waterman.

And a very special thanks goes to our good friend Bill Maul for believing in this project and to our two favorite stars on the roster, Sophie Nash and Kathy Zullo.

The Lineup

Raiders of the Lost Archives ix

Pitcher Loses Game—After He Retires! 1
...and Other Astounding Pitching Stories

Braves Play on Graves of Dead Horses! 21
...and Other Shocking Stories of the Bizarre

Fastest 9-Inning Game in History—Only 31 Minutes! 41
...and Other Stories of Unbelievable Games

Angels Take Batting Practice in Hotel Lobby! 53
...and Other Weird Batting Stories

Catcher Picks Off Runner—with a Potato! 63
...and Other Stories of Incredible Plays

The Uniform Number from Hell! 77
...and Other Unusual Stories of Uniforms and Equipment

Foul Ball Starts Fire—in Fan's Pocket! 85
...and Other Stories of Freaky Casualties

Nervous Runner Turns Home Run Into Double Play! 99
...and Other Startling Baserunning Stories

Booing Philly Fans Drive Dodgers Pitcher from Mound! 107
...and Other Outrageous Fan Stories

Manager Fires Himself! 121
...and Other Stories of Managerial Madness

Umpire Escapes Angry Mob—By Playing Dead! 131
...and Other Wild Stories About the Men in Blue

Dodgers Executive Trades His Own Son! 139
...and Other Stories of Outlandish Deals

9-Year-Old Plays in Pro Game! 145
...and Other Stories of Odd Occurrences

RAIDERS OF THE LOST ARCHIVES

For years we have tracked down and written over a thousand stories about the wackiest and most embarrassing moments in sports history in our *Hall of Shame* book series.

But while researching the offbeat side of sports, we also uncovered bizarre, weird, and strange stories that didn't quite fit into our *Hall of Shame* books. Stories like:

- The woman who once batted in a major league game.
- The death curse that haunts the California Angels.
- The future Hall of Famer who masqueraded as a female ballplayer.
- The game between a team of one-armed men and a squad of one-legged players.

We realized we were discovering the lost stories of sports. So we continued to sift through the yellowed pages of old newspapers and magazines, scour journals left forgotten on dusty museum shelves, and study box scores and records spanning a century of baseball. The more of these incredible-but-true accounts that we found, the more we felt like "the raiders of the lost archives."

Now we have collected the best of these lost stories and put them in a different kind of baseball book. On the following pages, you'll read some of the most astonishing true-life stories in baseball history from the teenage girl who struck out Babe Ruth to the major league outfielder who played in a bathrobe; from the witch doctor Houston hired to end the club's jinx to the home run ball that traveled more than 100 miles.

Because these untold stories are so sensational, we thought it would be fun to present them in a sensational way—in an outrageous mini-tabloid format complete with attention-grabbing headlines and eye-catching photos.

As you read these astounding stories, you might wonder if these accounts are really true. Did a UFO actually boost a slugger's career? Did the hypnotic eyes of a player wreck his career? Did a pitcher really get thrown in jail for walking four batters in a row?

Yes, they are all true. ***Believe it ...or else!***

Pitcher Loses Game — After He Retires!

...And Other Astounding Pitching Stories

TEENAGE GIRL STRIKES OUT BABE RUTH!

...and whiffs iron man Lou Gehrig on three straight pitches

Mighty home run slugger Babe Ruth was struck out by a 17-year-old girl!

Amazingly, the sensational teenage hurler then fanned the next hitter, Lou Gehrig—"the Pride of the Yankees"—to the astonishment of players and fans alike.

This incredible feat occurred on April 2, 1931, in a spring training exhibition game between the awesome New York Yankees and a minor-league Tennessee team, the Chattanooga Lookouts of the Southern Association.

The female fireballer was Virne Beatrice "Jackie" Mitchell, a 5-foot, 5-inch, 130-pound lefthander who became the first woman ever to play professional baseball with a men's team. She was signed by Lookouts owner Joe Engel, who figured that sending a girl out to the mound to face the Yankees' "Murderers' Row" would be a sure-fire way to fill his 4,000-seat ball park. He was right. Engel Stadium was Standing Room Only.

Ruth was not happy at the prospect of batting against a girl. "I don't know what's going to happen if they begin to let women in baseball," he told reporters before the game. "Of course, they will never make good because they are too delicate. It would kill them to play every day."

Jackie, who did not start the game, faced only three Yankees. The first was Ruth, who in the previous year had walloped a league-leading 49 homers and batted a hefty .359. As he stepped into the batter's box, he tipped his cap to the pretty teenager. Jackie had only one pitch—a sinker that took a nasty drop just as it reached the plate. She

The Babe threw his bat down in disgust and stalked back to the dugout

had learned the pitch from Brooklyn Dodgers hurler Dazzy Vance, who was a neighbor when she lived in Memphis.

Jackie's first pitch was high and outside for ball one. Then she reared back and fired again. This time, the Babe swung hard, but hit nothing but air. The crowd went wild.

Ruth stepped out of the batter's box and glared at Jackie. It was embarrassing for the great Bambino to whiff on a pitch thrown by a girl. He ignored the good-natured catcalls from his own dugout as he stepped back into the box. Jackie's next pitch was outside for ball two.

On the next pitch, Ruth whipped his bat with blinding speed, but again he missed for strike two. The bench-

YANKEE KILLER: Lou Gehrig (left) and Babe Ruth study the pitching form of Jackie Mitchell, the amazing young gal who fanned both superstars.

jockeying intensified as Babe testily turned to the plate umpire and demanded a new ball. This was getting downright humiliating. He dug his left foot deep into the dirt of the batter's box and slowly, menacingly waved his bat, determined not to let some fresh-faced girl show him up.

Jackie's next pitch looked high to Ruth so he kept his bat on his shoulder. But at the last possible moment, the pitch dropped to belt high and zipped across the middle of the plate. The Babe stood there in disbelief as the umpire yelled, "Strike three! Yer out!" Four thousand fans rose to their feet in a thundering roar. His face turning red from embarrassment, Ruth threw down his bat in disgust and stalked back to the dugout, passing a grinning Lou Gehrig on the way.

But moments later, Gehrig wasn't smiling either. He swung hard at three straight pitches from Jackie and missed them all. Unlike Ruth, Gehrig acknowledged Jackie's amazing pitching with a nod and then quietly headed back to the dugout with bat in hand.

After striking out the two superstars, Jackie's control abandoned her and she walked Yankees shortstop Tony Lazzeri. She was then taken out of the game. That set off a standing ovation that lasted for nearly ten minutes as the excited fans cheered themselves hoarse.

When the din died down, many fans wondered if they had witnessed history or a setup. But later, when questioned by reporters, both Ruth and Gehrig asserted that it was no fix. Jackie was simply a much better pitcher than they had expected.

"I was on cloud nine for days after that," recalled Jackie, who died in 1987. "I was the happiest girl in the world." ◇

Phil Niekro was the best pitcher in the National League in 1979—and also the worst. Incredibly, Niekro, of the Atlanta Braves, led the National League that year in both wins and losses. He won 21 but lost 20.

3

Owner Has Hurler Arrested For Walking 4 in a Row!

Pitcher Saul Rogovin was arrested and jailed during a game—for the heinous crime of walking four batters in a row!

The 24-year-old righthander received the shock of his baseball career when he played for Caracas in a 1947 Winter League game in Venezuela.

Rogovin, who later pitched eight years in the major leagues, was a hurler for the Buffalo Bisons of the International League when he decided to join the Venezuela Baseball Club in Caracas during the offseason. He wanted to get some more experience—but not the kind he received during a home night game on November 17, 1947.

"I had been ordered by the owner to

SAUL ROGOVIN was put in jail for a poor performance.

The cops hustled the hapless hurler off to a Caracas jail

pitch with one day's rest," Rogovin recalled. "I didn't want to do it because I had been pitching quite a bit and my arm needed rest between starts. But he insisted."

So the weary-armed hurler dutifully went out to the mound and proceeded to walk the first four batters he faced. Rogovin was then yanked from the game. But no sooner had he stepped into the dugout then club owner Oscar Yanes read him the riot act for his poor pitching performance.

When Rogovin tried to explain that his arm was tired and he shouldn't have been pitching in the first place, Yanes refused to listen to reason and he flew off the handle. He summoned four local policemen and ordered them to arrest the stunned Rogovin. Without considering what possible charges might stick on the pitcher, the cops hustled the hapless hurler off to a Caracas jail.

Rogovin was detained for several hours and finally released about midnight after Yanes came to his senses and declined to press charges—as if there were any.

"The next day I told Yanes that I was through playing for him and that I was going home," said Rogovin. "We had some words and then he apologized. In fact, he even gave me a raise. So I stayed on a few more months, but my pitching was only mediocre back then.

"I learned one thing about winter ball in Venezuela. It was a whole other world where they did things a lot differently than in the States." ◇

4

Pitcher makes biggest save of his career—a fan's life!

Texas Rangers pitcher Doc Medich lived up to his name when he made the biggest save of his career —a fan's life.

Medich, a 29-year-old veteran hurler, was planning a career as an orthopedic surgeon when his playing days were over. During the offseason prior to the 1978 season, he had finished his first year as a resident physician at Allegheny General Hospital in Pittsburgh.

His medical training made him a lifesaver on July 17, 1978, shortly before a game against the Orioles at Baltimore's Memorial Stadium. Medich was loosening up, running wind sprints in right field, when he heard an emergency call for a doctor over the public address system.

Medich rushed from the field into the stands a few rows behind the Orioles' dugout where fan Germain Languth of Pasadena, Maryland, was suffering a heart attack. The man had no discernable pulse and was rapidly losing color when Medich arrived. The pitcher worked feverishly for more than half an hour, giving the 61-year-old fan mouth-to-mouth resuscitation and heart massage.

When paramedics arrived, Medich attached tubes and lines for the administration of medication and electrical shock. Finally, the fast-acting pitcher was able to generate a pulse stable enough for Languth to be moved to a hospital.

Medich was near exhaustion when the incident was over and asked for time to recover before speaking to reporters about his lifesaving efforts.

"Things were kind of disorganized when I got there," Medich recalled. "He wasn't getting enough oxygen. I

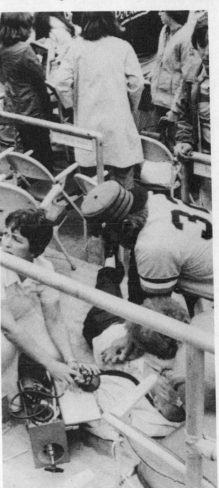

DOC MEDICH applies first aid to a fan who suffered a heart attack.

started giving orders and people started following them."

It was not the first time Medich had been involved in such a case—he had already resuscitated 25 heart attack victims in the hospital during his residency. And it was also not the first time he had been called on at the ball park to save a fan.

Two years earlier, when he played for the Pittsburgh Pirates, Medich tried to save the life of a heart attack victim before a game in Philadelphia.

But the fan died despite the best efforts of Medich and the emergency personnel.

Fortunately for Languth, he survived the heart attack . . . thanks to a save from pitching physician Doc Medich. ◇

A Head of Beer

A Chicago White Sox fan keeps his cool with a "no hands" beer break while rooting for his team, which was playing the Boston Red Sox at Comiskey Park in 1985.

Giants Drum Phillies Pitcher Out of the League—Literally

The New York Giants literally drummed Philadelphia Phillies pitcher Harry Coveleski out of the league.

As a rookie, Coveleski wrecked the Giants' chances of winning the 1908 pennant by beating them three times at the end of the season. Because of this extraordinary feat, Coveleski was given the nickname "The Giant Killer."

The New Yorkers, who finished one game behind the first-place Chicago Cubs, blamed Coveleski for their failure to win the pennant and steamed all winter. They wanted revenge.

During the offseason, Cincinnati Reds scout Tacks Ashenbach, who knew Coveleski from his days growing up in Shamokin, Pennsylvania, gave Giants manager John McGraw the secret to beating Coveleski.

"Mac," said Ashenbach, "I'm surprised you let that big guy beat you out of the pennant. I can give you the prescription to use every time he pitches against you. All you have to do is imitate a snare drum."

"What are you trying to do, kid me?" asked McGraw.

"Try it," said the scout.

Sure enough, the very first time Coveleski faced New York the next year, the entire Giants' bench struck up a chorus of "rat-a-tat-tat, rat-a-tat-tat." The coaches on the field picked it up too . . . "rat-a-tat-tat, rat-a-tat-tat."

Coveleski started a slow burn and got wilder and wilder as the drum chorus continued. With his control gone and his concentration shattered, the flustered hurler was finally yanked from the game in the fourth inning.

Word spread like wildfire throughout the league and soon everywhere Coveleski went, he heard the maddening "rat-a-tat-tat, rat-a-tat-tat." He became so rattled on the mound that he didn't even finish out the year in the bigs. After posting a 6-10 record, Coveleski was shipped back to the minors and didn't return until 1914 except for a few brief appearances in 1910. In fact, he never beat the Giants again once they learned how to mess with his mind.

> **The maddening sound of "rat-a-tat-tat" drove Coveleski nuts every time he pitched**

The drumming charade psyched out Coveleski because it triggered memories of a lost love.

Shortly before his baseball days, Coveleski had fallen head over heels in love with a young woman in Shamokin whose whole life revolved around music and local bands. Coveleski wasn't musically inclined, but she made it clear that if he wanted to win her heart, he would have to learn how to play an instrument.

So Coveleski took up the snare drum. He practiced and practiced until he was ready to perform in the annual local concert. However, during the show, Coveleski missed his cue and came in on a violin solo and almost wrecked the concert. He promptly was dismissed—by both the band director and the girl. The young man's heart was further broken when the gal eventually ran off with a local drummer.

That's why the sound of "rat-a-tat-tat, rat-a-tat-tat " drove Coveleski nuts when he pitched. But fortunately for the hurler, his skin grew thicker over time and he ignored all further attempts to psych him out. After spending four years in the minors, Coveleski—the brother of Hall of Famer Stanley Coveleski—returned to the majors. Pitching to beat the band, Coveleski, now with the Detroit Tigers, silenced his detractors and their bats by posting three straight seasons of 20-plus wins. He had a career mark of 81-55. ◇

Hurler's Tongue Swells Up...

Phils Smear Hot Liniment On Ball to Foil Spitballer

Pittsburgh Pirates spitballer Marty O'Toole got a taste of his own medicine when a player on the opposing team loaded up the ball with burning-hot liniment that set the hurler's tongue on fire.

In 1912—eight years before the spitball was declared illegal—O'Toole faced the Philadelphia Phillies who were fed up with his spitters. They were especially vexed by his disgusting practice of holding the ball up to his face, hiding it with his glove and licking it with his tongue.

Phillies first baseman Fred Luderus decided to take matters into his own hands. He figured that if the pitcher could use a foreign substance on the ball, so could he. So Luderus took a small tube of powerful liniment onto the field with him and every time he handled the ball, he rubbed the fiery hot salve on it.

Within a few innings, O'Toole's tongue was so inflamed, raw, and painful that he had to leave the game.

When Pittsburgh manager Fred Clarke discovered what Luderus had done, the skipper was livid and issued a formal statement denouncing the player. "This liniment is the most powerful known," said Clarke. "Suppose a man should get a little of it on his hands and rub his eye. He could be blind for hours."

But Philadelphia manager Red Dooin issued his own statement, claiming the liniment was used merely to protect the health of his players. "That ball may be carrying the germs of any one of many contagious diseases," argued Dooin. "So we put disinfectant on it whenever we face a spitball pitcher like O'Toole. I do not see how we can be refused the privilege of protecting ourselves."

O'Toole knew he was licked and no longer used his tongue to load up the ball. ◇

★★★

Los Angeles Angels pitcher Paul Foytack holds the record for giving up the most consecutive home runs in one inning—four. He served up the gopher balls in a 1963 game against the Cleveland Indians.

8

Pitcher Loses Game —After He Retires!

Philadelphia Phillies hurler Jim Hearn lost a game—two months *after* **he retired from baseball!**

In fact, he was selling underwear when he was tagged with the loss.

When Hearn—who pitched from 1947 through 1959 for the St. Louis Cardinals, New York Giants, and Phillies—hung up his cleats for the last time, his lifetime record was 109 wins and 88 losses. But two months later, his record was changed to 89 losses. And it wasn't a scorekeeping error.

In 1959, Hearn's pitching career was at the end of the road. He appeared in only six games that year for the Phillies, all in relief, and wound up with an 0-2 record.

On May 10, Hearn pitched 1 1/3 innings in Pittsburgh against the Pirates, allowing two earned runs. He was the pitcher of record when the game was suspended in the ninth inning because of the Pennsylvania Sunday curfew law, which prohibited baseball from being played after 6 p.m. on the Sabbath. The Pirates were leading 6-4 at the time.

The game was scheduled to be resumed two months later, on July 21, which was the next time the clubs were slated to meet in Pittsburgh. But on May 22, the Phillies released Hearn. So the 38-year-old hurler retired from baseball and returned to his hometown

JIM HEARN was tagged with a loss two months after retiring.

of Atlanta where he became an underwear salesman for Van Heusen.

The suspended game was finally completed on July 21, and the Phillies lost 6-4. Since Hearn was still the pitcher of record, he was saddled with the loss—two months after he retired from baseball. ◇

Harley "Doc" Parker hurled the worst-pitched game in major league history. On June 21, 1901, the Cincinnati Reds' hurler gave up a record-shattering 26 hits—one homer, five doubles, and 20 singles—to the Brooklyn Dodgers. He also surrendered a National League high of 21 runs. The next day, Parker was released by the Reds.

Priest-to-Be Pitches for Tigers—And Loses 24-2

Al Travers took time out from his studies for the priesthood to pitch an historic game for the Detroit Tigers. But no amount of prayers could help him on the mound—and he was clobbered 24-2.

In his wildest dreams, Travers never expected—or even wanted—to pitch in the majors. He was drafted by the Tigers on May 18, 1912, in a desperate move to field a team of strike-breakers.

It was all because of Detroit star Ty Cobb.

Three days earlier in New York, Cobb charged into the stands after a heckler and beat him up. The fan was so badly hurt that American League president Ban Johnson suspended Cobb indefinitely without a hearing.

The Detroit players were incensed. They felt the fan was so verbally abusive and vicious that Cobb had a right to go after him. So they told Johnson they would not play until Cobb was reinstated.

Johnson threatened to suspend the players and fine team owner Frank Navin $5,000 for every game that the Tigers missed.

To avoid the fine, the owner instructed manager Hughie Jennings to round up a standby team in case the Tigers players went on strike at their next game in Philadelphia against the Athletics. Jennings turned to *Philadelphia Bulletin* reporter John Nolan for help.

So Nolan went to the St. Joseph's College campus and recruited Travers, a 20-year-old junior. "I wasn't much of a ballplayer, and I had never actually pitched a full game in my life," recalled Travers. "I liked the sport, though, so when John asked me if I could round up 12 players, I agreed."

Nolan had assured him that they

"Napoleon got his at Waterloo, and I got mine at Shibe Park"

FATHER TRAVIS: Dubious debut.

wouldn't actually have to play. "He told me that it was all arranged with [A's president and manager] Connie Mack that the game would be called off if the players struck. But they had to have 12 men in uniform to avoid the fine.

"So I went down to 23rd and Columbia and rounded up a bunch of guys who were standing around on the corner."

Everything went according to plan at Shibe Park—for awhile. The real Tigers took infield practice, but when Johnson refused to lift Cobb's suspension, they went into the clubhouse, took their uniforms off, and left.

"We put the uniforms on," said Travers. "We just thought we'd go out and appear. We never thought we'd play a game."

But when Connie Mack saw the ragged bunch on the field, he smelled an easy victory—and pulled a doublecross. He refused to cancel the game.

"I became the pitcher because the pitcher was going to get $50, and the rest of the players $10 each," Travers explained. "We were nothing but a bunch of nondescripts. It's a wonder we ever got them out."

Two Tigers coaches were pressed into service—42-year-old Joe Sugden, who played first base, and 49-year-old James McGuire, who caught.

"I was throwing slow curves—the only pitch I really knew—and the A's weren't used to them," said Travers. "The score was only 6 2 in the fifth inning. I had pretty fair success until they started bunting on us." Since Travers knew nothing about fielding bunts and the third baseman had never played baseball before, the A's had a field day.

Not counting the mental miscues, the ersatz Tigers made nine errors. Travers gave up 25 hits and 24 runs, only 14 of which were earned.

The amateurs' performance was so awful that the Detroit owner knew he couldn't put them on the field again.

Meanwhile, the public was in an uproar—siding with Cobb—and the real Tigers still refused to play.

Cobb settled the issue by urging his teammates to give up their strike. They did after AL president Johnson reduced Cobb's suspension to 10 days and fined him $50.

Al Travers, meanwhile, traded his baseball flannels for the cloth of the clergy and eventually became a Catholic priest. "Father Travers made history just like Napoleon," he said. "He got his at Waterloo . . . and I got mine at Shibe Park." ◇

Pitcher Exorcises His Glove —And Wins!

An Iona College pitcher broke a personal seven-game losing streak by turning to a bizarre remedy— exorcism!

In 1988, Phil McKiverkin cast about for some explanation of why he was mired in such a depressing and embarrassing string of pitching failures. He decided his glove was to blame. "It was a Bret Saberhagen model," McKiverkin said. "I had bought it new for the season, but I just couldn't win with it."

Was the glove evil? Did it possess some demonic power? Said the hurler, "The only answer was exorcism."

Before a home game on April 19, 1988, McKiverkin and several teammates gathered along the left field foul line where he doused the glove with alcohol and set it afire.

While the glove burned, his teammates chanted incantations—in Hebrew, Italian, and other tongues. Whatever they chanted, it worked.

The very next day, McKiverkin took the mound with a borrowed glove and got credit for a win in relief. It wasn't a very pretty win—Iona beat Brooklyn College 26-14—but it was a win nonetheless.

As for the exorcism of his glove, McKiverkin said, "I'm grateful to my teammates. They could have burned my right arm instead." ◇

Expos Sign 6-Fingered Pitcher

Of all the Montreal Expos' pitching prospects in 1991, Antonio Alfonseca proved to have the best grasp of the game. That's because he has six fingers on each hand!

Not only does he have 12 fingers, he also has 12 toes, which add up to the reason why his friends in the Dominican Republic, where he grew up, gave him his nickname—"The Octopus."

"I think God gave me more fingers and toes because He wanted to show that I'm special and that I will be somebody someday," said Antonio, the son of a poor sugar cane cutter. Neither his parents nor his five brothers and sisters have extra digits, but his grandfather also had 12 fingers and toes. "He was the original Octopus," Antonio said.

Expos scout Jesus Alou sees hundreds of Dominican kids each year, but he never saw one like Antonio before.

"One of the things I look for in a

...He's nicknamed 'The Octopus'

pitcher is big hands," said Alou. "In order to find that out I make sure I shake hands with every kid who comes to our training camp. When I shook hands with Antonio, I felt something funny there. I looked and I just said, 'Oh my goodness.' "

The 6-foot, 4-inch, 18-year-old rookie, who throws 90-mile-an-hour fastballs, "has great talent," said Frank Wren, the Expos' scout who signed Antonio. "He throws very hard and has a good assortment of pitches."

The extra finger has not given Antonio an advantage—yet. "I've tried to figure out what to do with it," he admitted. "But so far, I haven't been able to put it to use."

Alou said, "What the heck, he's getting older. He might come up with something using that extra finger one of these days. Meanwhile, 'The Octopus' has all the tools to be a major leaguer."

Despite his extra finger, Antonio doesn't need a custom-made glove. "I just put my two little fingers in the regular glove's last finger," he said.

"Many people laughed at me because of my extra fingers and toes. And the first American team that tried to sign me—the New York Yankees—wanted me to have an operation to remove them. I refused to sign with the Yankees because I don't want my extra fingers and toes cut off. I've never felt ashamed of them. They're God's gift to me." ◇

ANTONIO ALFONSECA shows off his unusual six-fingered grip.

Hurler Throws No-Hitter —One Hour After the Game Ends!

JEFF TESREAU didn't know he had pitched a no-hitter.

New York Giants pitcher Jeff Tesreau threw a no-hitter against the Philadelphia Phillies—but didn't know it until an hour after the game. That's when the official scorer changed the one hit the hurler had given up to an error.

The controversy focused on a popup lofted by Phillies leadoff batter Dode Paskert in the first inning of the game played in Philadelphia on Sept. 6, 1912. It was a short pop fly between first and home. Giants first baseman Fred Merkle and catcher Art Wilson almost collided going after the ball, which fell just inside the foul line. Official scorer Stoney McLinn called the play a hit and the game continued without a second thought to the ruling.

The Phillies never came close to getting a hit again. Tesreau twirled a masterful game, giving up two walks on his way to a 3-0 shutout and an apparent one-hitter.

While the Giants were in the clubhouse savoring their win, reporters in the press box were having a spirited debate. Believing Tesreau had been robbed of a no-hitter by a bad call from the official scorer, several New York sportswriters challenged McLinn's ruling on Paskert's popup.

"Merkle touched the ball," the New Yorkers insisted. "It should have been an error."

Other witnesses insisted they could see daylight between Merkle's glove and the ball. Philadelphia manager Red Dooin, who was coaching first at the time, claimed Merkle never touched it. But Merkle told the scorer the ball tipped his glove.

Tesreau, who seemed nonchalant about the flap, said, "I don't care. I won the game and that's all I care about."

Finally, about an hour after the game ended, McLinn changed the scoring from a hit to an error, and Tesreau received credit for the no-hitter, the first in the league that year. ◇

Pirate Hurls 12 Perfect Innings—And Loses!!

In the most astounding pitching performance in major league history, Pittsburgh Pirates hurler Harvey Haddix threw 12 perfect innings in one unforgettable game—and lost!

After setting down 36 straight Milwaukee Braves without a man reaching first, Haddix made one lone pitching mistake in the 13th inning and suffered an incredible, heartbreaking 1-0 defeat.

Ironically, when Haddix warmed up for the visiting Pirates the night of May 29, 1959, he felt sluggish. He thought his fastball didn't have its usual "pop" and that his curve wasn't breaking sharply enough. To make matters worse, he was fighting a cold.

"I don't feel sharp," the veteran, 5-foot, 9-inch southpaw told manager Danny Murtaugh before the game. "I'll just have to do the best I can as long as I can."

It was impossible to perform any better. At the end of nine innings, Haddix had pitched a perfect game. But in a cruel twist of fate, he pitched flawlessly on a night when his teammates' bats were silent. Though the Pirates had several scoring opportunities, they were being shut out by Braves hurler Lew Burdette.

Haddix continued to pitch his heart out. Stunned fans and players watched in amazement as the little lefty mowed down the Braves through the 10th, 11th and 12th innings—36 up and 36 down. What made the feat even more remarkable was that Milwaukee, which

HARVEY HADDIX walks off field with manager Danny Murtaugh.

finished second that year, had an awesome lineup that featured such sluggers as Hank Aaron, Eddie Mathews, Joe Adcock, and Del Crandall.

But even though the Pirates threatened to score time and again, they still couldn't punch across one measly run.

Haddix's perfect game finally ended in the bottom of the 13th . . . and it wasn't even his fault. Leadoff hitter Felix Mantilla hit a ground ball to third baseman Don Hoak, who threw wildly into the dirt at first. Mantilla was safe on the error and became the Braves' very first baserunner. Haddix then intentionally walked Aaron.

Now came Haddix's only mistake of the night—a pitch that crushed his dreams of a no-hitter, a shutout, and a win. Joe Adcock nailed a fastball that barely cleared the center field fence for a dramatic, game-ending home run. Joyous Milwaukee fans began filing out of County Stadium, thinking the Braves had won 3-0.

But in the spirit of this unbelievable night, the four-bagger was no ordinary homer. In fact, it turned out to be a double instead.

On the hit, Mantilla trotted home with the winning run. But Aaron thought the ball was still inside the park. When he saw Mantilla score, Aaron jogged off the base path and toward the dugout, thinking the game

had ended. Meanwhile, Adcock continued his home run trot until he touched the plate.

When the Braves realized what Aaron had done, they rushed him back out onto the field, where he completed his jog around the bases. Adcock re-ran them again as well, this time staying behind Aaron.

Too late, the umpire ruled. Adcock was out for passing Aaron on the bases—thus, turning his home run into a double.

But Aaron's run still counted, the ump said, making the final score 2-0.

However, the next day, National League President Warren Giles ruled the umpire was in error in allowing Aaron to score. Giles ruled that since Adcock was out and got credit for only a double, Aaron couldn't have scored from first. That made the official final score 1-0.

Not that it mattered to Haddix. He had pitched the greatest game ever in the major leagues . . . and lost. ◇

The Case of the Invisible Catcher

No, that's not a phantom catcher holding a ball and mitt. Just seconds before this photo was taken during a 1956 college game, Southern Tech runner Lee Stringer slammed into South Georgia catcher Charlie Williams, knocking loose the ball and the glove.

Pitcher yanked from showers —and then sent to the mound

LARRY FRENCH pitched with soap squishing out of his shirt.

Instead of being pulled from the mound and sent to the showers, Pittsburgh Pirates pitcher Larry French was pulled from the showers and sent to the mound.

On July 12, 1933, the Pirates were enjoying an 8-0 laugher over the visiting Boston Braves as the game headed into the top of the ninth inning. With starting pitcher Heinie Meine cruising along, French, who was relaxing in the bullpen, figured he could sneak off to the clubhouse early.

It's hot, I'm tired, and there's no chance they're going to need me, he thought. *Wouldn't it be great to be the first one in the showers and take a nice, quiet, long soaking?* French then left the bullpen, inconspicuously slipped into the clubhouse, and went quickly into the showers.

He was soaped from head to foot when he heard the clubhouse boy yell, "You're wanted in the bullpen, Mr. French."

"Go on, kid," French snarled. "Beat it. I'm staying right where I am. They don't need me and you know it."

The boy ran from the room and French started rinsing off. Suddenly he heard another shout, looked up, and saw a teammate poking his head into the showers. "What do you want?" French snapped.

"Forget about the bullpen, Larry," said the teammate. "You've got to get out on the diamond. And hurry up. Boston has already scored six runs in the ninth and they're still batting.

(Manager George) Gibson is yelling for you to get your butt out there now!"

French made a mad dash for his uniform, threw it on, and raced to the mound, with soap bubbles still squishing out of his uniform. Incredibly, the Braves were now trailing by only 8-7 and had a runner on third with one out. Still in shock over being pulled from the showers, French gave up a game-trying sacrifice fly to the first batter he faced and then retired the next Brave.

After the Pirates failed to score in their half of the frame, French mowed down the Braves in the top of the tenth and got the win when Pittsburgh pushed across a run in the bottom of the inning.

Thus, Larry French became the only pitcher in history to win a game after being pulled—from the showers.

Browns Pitcher 'Owned' Ruth...

The Man Who Struck Fear In the Babe

No pitcher struck more fear into the heart of Babe Ruth than a rookie hurler named Hub "Shucks" Pruett of the St. Louis Browns.

In 1922, Pruett faced the feared slugger 13 times—and struck him out ten times.

Pruett, a skinny 21-year-old southpaw who signed with the Browns out of the University of Missouri, first pitched against the Bambino in relief on April 22, 1922. "When I went out to the mound, I didn't know who he was," recalled Pruett. "All I knew was that he batted lefthanded."

The rookie struck out Babe on three pitches. And it was no fluke. He fanned the slugger nine of the next 12 times he faced him.

Pruett, who was nicknamed "Shucks" because that was the strongest word in his vocabulary, always whiffed the Bambino with his money pitch, a screwball. The press labeled it "the pitch that bamboozled the Babe."

Late in the season, Ruth retaliated by clubbing a home run off the rookie.

HUB PRUETT fanned Ruth 10 out of the first 13 times he faced him.

"I wanted to throw the screwball, but catcher Hank Severeid shook me off and called for the curve," Pruett recalled. "I hung the curve and Ruth hit

17

the ball far over the right field wall." Pruett still won 5-1.

During the three years he pitched in the American League, Pruett struck out the Bambino 15 times in 30 at-bats. Ruth walked eight times, hit a sacrifice fly, grounded out twice, and collected four hits. Against Pruett, Babe—a .342 lifetime hitter—batted an anemic .190.

Pruett suffered a sore arm in his rookie year and never reached his full potential. He posted a career record of 29-48 with an ERA of 4.63 in seven years in the bigs.

Ironically, Pruett's uncanny pitching success against the Babe helped the pitcher become a physician. Pruett played baseball only as a means of paying his way through medical school in the offseason. With the money he made in the majors, he earned his medical degree in eight years.

"My won-lost record doesn't look too impressive," he said. "What got me a reputation and kept me in baseball were those dramatic strikeouts of Ruth. I owe him a lot."

Pruett never spoke to Ruth during his career. "At the ball park, we'd pass each other without speaking. But every once in a while, he did something that gave me a kick. He'd wink at me.

"I only spoke to him once in my life. I met him in 1948 in St. Louis at a baseball dinner. I went up and introduced myself and said, 'Thanks, Babe, for putting me through medical school. If it hadn't been for you, nobody would ever have heard of me.'

"The Babe said, 'I'm glad there weren't many more like you. I never would have gotten by in the major leagues. If I had anything to do with making you a doctor, I'm glad.' " ◇

Pitching for Peanuts

Achille the elephant gets ready to throw out the first ball of the 1989 season. The pachyderm performed the ceremonial duty before an Opening Night game between the visiting Mariners and the A's.

He Chooses Revolution Over Baseball...

Giants Offer Fidel Castro Contract and Bonus to Pitch

Before becoming the bearded, iron-fisted dictator of Cuba, Fidel Castro was offered a contract to pitch for the New York Giants.

In 1948, Castro was a clean-shaven, 21-year-old pre-law student at the University of Havana and a star hurler for the school's baseball team with a 9-2 record. He also pitched for various amateur league teams around the city.

It wasn't long before Castro caught the eyes of several major league scouts, including the Giants' Alex Pompez. His scouting report stated that Castro ". . . is a smart prospect and throws a good ball . . . not always hard, but smart. He has good control and should be considered seriously . . . Castro is a prospect."

The Pittsburgh Pirates and Washington Senators also expressed interest in the Cuban hurler. A Senators scouting report said Castro ". . . is a big, powerful young man. His fastball is not great, but passable . . . He uses his head and can win that way for us, too. He is . . . a definite prospect . . . to sign."

Another Giants scouting report called Castro a polite, stable, well-spoken gentleman "more serious than many other local players."

And better than most. Pitching against a team of touring major leaguers in November, 1948, Castro impressed the Americans by striking out four of the 16 batters he faced. He gave up no runs on three hits.

The following spring, when Castro won his first five games for the University of Havana, the Giants offered him a standard contract with a $5,000 signing bonus. After mulling it

STRONG ARM MAN: Fidel Castro winds up during game in Cuba.

over for a few days, Castro stunned the club by turning it down.

"We couldn't believe he turned us down," recalled Pompez. "Nobody from Latin America said no before.

"He told me that helping people with the law would be his career while baseball would be his hobby."

Castro never showed the scouts any clue that he would one day be the most despised tyrant of the Western Hemisphere. When Castro came to power in 1959 and turned Cuba into a communist state, the Giants were shocked to learn he was the same polite young man they had tried to sign.

Recalled Horace Stoneham, former president of the Giants, "If he had taken our offer and gone into pro baseball, there's no question in our minds that he would have made it to the major leagues." ◇

19

Softball Pitching Star A Big Flop in the Pros

Bob Fesler—known as the "King of the Softball Pitchers" in the 1950s—was dethroned in his debut in professional baseball.

As a softball pitcher, Fesler mowed batters down with six varieties of curves and speed to burn. He was so impressive that in 1955 the Seattle Rainiers, of the AAA Pacific Coast League, signed him up.

In batting practice, Fesler showed an uncanny ability to bewilder Seattle batters with his windmill underhanded motions. So on August 10, in the midst of a pennant race, Rainiers manager Fred Hutchinson announced his starting pitcher would be the softball sensation.

More than 14,000 fans showed up at Seattle's Sick Stadium to watch the softballer throw hardballs against the San Francisco Seals in the first game of a twinbill.

In his debut, Fesler fanned San

...Lasts One Day!

Francisco's leadoff batter on three straight pitches. Immortality seemed to be beckoning. The fans' hopes rose. Could a great softball pitcher dominate baseball players?

Nope. The strikeout was the highlight of Fesler's performance. He then gave up a walk, a wild pitch, a balk, another walk, a wild pitch, a single, a walk, a three-run double, and a walk. Hutchinson had seen enough and gave Fesler the hook after pitching just 1/3 of an inning. The Seals tallied five runs in the frame and won 5-3.

Fesler got one more chance to pitch. In the second game that day, he came back in as a reliever and struck out two men with the bases loaded. However, he also gave up four walks, three singles, and a home run.

Fesler never pitched in professional baseball again. ◇

★★★

Tommy John Laughs Himself Out of the Game

Chicago White Sox pitcher Tommy John thought an umpire's call was so funny that he laughed himself right off the mound and into the showers.

In a 1968 game, John was pitching to Baltimore Orioles batter Don Buford with flamboyant umpire Ron Luciano behind the plate. With nobody on base in the fourth inning, John went into his windup and accidentally dropped the ball behind him. But as a lark, he went ahead and completed his delivery.

"Stee-rike!" the umpire bellowed,

going along with the joke.

But Buford didn't think the invisible pitch was so funny. He turned and glared at Luciano, who promptly said, "No pitch."

While Buford wasn't smiling, John broke up laughing on the mound. In fact, he couldn't stop laughing. He walked Buford and the next two batters as well. Then he gave up a double and was given the hook. John was still laughing on his way to the showers.

Braves Play on Graves of Dead Horses!

...And Other Shocking Stories of the Bizarre

L.A. Dodger Reveals:

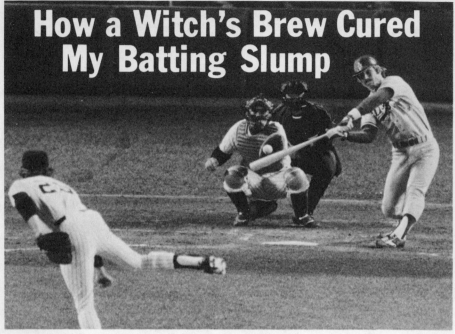

How a Witch's Brew Cured My Batting Slump

RON CEY: His newfound supernatural power ended his batting slump.

For Los Angeles Dodgers third baseman Ron Cey, that old black magic had him in its spell.

During the last two weeks of the 1977 regular season, Cey fell into a terrible batting slump. Not until he sprinkled himself with a magic potion concocted by a modern-day witch did he go on a hitting spree in the National League Championship Series, propelling the Dodgers into the World Series.

The good witch, Ruth Revzen, a self-described "nice little Jewish girl who makes potions," had brewed a bottle of a magical mixture for Cey after his wife appealed to her for help. At the time, Cey's hitting slump had stretched to 31 straight at-bats without a hit in the regular season.

Revzen created a strong-smelling concoction ("the most God-awful smelling stuff," said Cey) that was to be applied like cologne. All Cey had to do was breathe it, she said. The exact formula was a secret, but she said it came straight from the Bible.

"The smell is very potent," Revzen said. "The herbs involved in it work by getting inside your skin. The smell will influence you and set the glands going."

Cey, willing to try anything to break out of his slump, splashed the magic potion all over himself before donning his uniform for the opening game of the N.L.C.S. against the Philadelphia Phillies. Incredibly, in his first at-bat in the playoffs, Cey whacked a sharp single to left field, ending his awful hitting slump. What happened in the seventh inning was even more astounding. Cey belted a grand-slam home run!

"There's no doubt that the potion worked wonders," said Revzen. Added

Cey after the game, "I really wasn't a believer, but I am now."

In the playoffs, which the Dodgers won three games to one, Cey led the team in hitting with a .308 batting average, scored four runs, and drove in four runs.

Cey wasn't the only player helped by Revzen's magic that year. Chicago White Sox pitcher Steve Stone said he used her potion with amazing results. He went from a dismal 3-6 record with the Cubs the previous year to a career-high 15 wins with the Sox.

"The potion sure worked for me," he said.

Revzen traced her psychic powers back four generations to Romania and the home of Dracula. Her great, great grandfather was a mystic rabbi; her great, great grandmother made crystal balls.

"Jewish magic is the strongest there is," she said. ◊

DEATH CURSE HAUNTS ANGELS

No team has been as cursed as the California Angels.

During a chillingly hellacious period in the 1960s and 1970s, the Angels suffered more tragic fatalities and career-ending accidents than any team in major league baseball. In every case, the victims were young, up-and-coming stars.

Here is the Angels' frightening roster of death:

• 1965—Promising young pitcher Dick Wantz died of a brain tumor just weeks after pitching his first and only major league game.

• 1972—Infielder Chico Ruiz died from a car wreck a mile from his home.

• 1974—Pitcher Bruce Heinbechner lost his life in an auto accident during spring training shortly after learning he had made the team.

• 1977—Shortstop Mike Miley was killed in an auto accident.

• 1978—Outfielder Lyman Bostock, a career .311 hitter, was shot and killed in a family dispute.

• 1989—After compiling a 5-2 record for the Angels the previous season, relief pitcher Donnie Moore committed suicide.

During the 1960s and 1970s, several Angels suffered accidents that were fatal to their careers.

Ken McBride was an All-Star pitcher in 1963, heading toward a 20-win season when his auto was rear-ended and he sustained a back injury. Pitching with a bad back, McBride lost 10 games in a row and had no choice but to give up the game he loved.

In 1968, star pitcher Minnie Rojas, after three straight winning seasons for the Angels, suffered a severed spine in a car accident and he never pitched again.

Outfielder Bobby Valentine's career was ruined when he crashed into the center field wall at Anaheim Stadium in 1973 and broke his leg in two places.

In 1974, promising catcher Charlie Sands injured his knee in the final exhibition game of spring training. He never fully recovered and was forced to quit baseball. ◊

PALL BEARERS: Managers and coaches carry the coffin to its burial site.

Indians Bury 1948 Pennant in Stadium Grave

"... And may it rest in peace."

With those solemn words, the Cleveland Indians' 1948 American League pennant was lowered in a freshly-dug grave behind the center field fence of Municipal Stadium.

A cardboard tombstone bearing the inscription, "Here lies the 1948 champs" marked the burial place.

The funeral—held before the Indians' final home night game of the 1949 season—was the brainchild of owner Bill Veeck, whose club finished a disappointing third place after winning the World Series the year before.

In reporting the ceremony of Sept. 23, 1949, *The Cleveland Plain Dealer* said: "Funeral services for the pennant, the symbol of a championship which died in Boston Tuesday after a long illness, were held before 29,646 stadium mourners who generally agreed the unprecedented stunt was a suitable way to view the passing of a pennant."

The funeral procession formed near the Cleveland bullpen in right field. Veeck, portraying the mortician in a high silk hat, dabbed his eyes with a handkerchief while perched atop a horse-drawn hearse.

Among the pallbearers were manager Lou Boudreau and coaches Bill McKechnie, Steve O'Neill, and Muddy Ruel. "Parson" Ruddie Schaffer, the club's business manager, read the last rights from the "bible of baseball"—*The Sporting News.*

While a band played a funeral dirge, the procession moved to the center field flagpole where the pennant was lowered and placed in a pine coffin. The pallbearers adorned the coffin with flowers and put it in the hearse.

With a "grief-stricken" Veeck in the driver's seat, the parson and pallbearers walked slowly behind the hearse as it circled the playing field. When it passed the Cleveland dugout, the Indians joined the procession of mourners.

The Indians' bats must have remained in mourning because the Tribe went out and lost that night 5-0 to the Detroit Tigers. ◇

24

Teammates Feared Him...

Player's 'Hypnotic Eyes' Destroy His Career

Billy Earle was an excellent hitter who could play most any position, yet he never lasted more than a year with a team. He played on 13 clubs in nine years—because his teammates were afraid of him . . . and his "hypnotic eyes."

Earle had a pair of piercing eyes that seemed to blaze with a strange light. When he looked at his teammates, they would get a strange, creepy feeling. No one could explain it nor could they point to any actual incident. But the players just didn't like Earle looking at them for fear they would fall under a bizarre trance.

In the 1880's and '90s, Earle developed not only a sharp batting eye, but a hypnotic one as well. Claiming he possessed "mesmeric powers," the press back then reported that Earle could hypnotize people to do most anything.

"I cannot describe how I am able to control these subjects," Earle told reporters. "I have failed only seven times experimenting with 115 people."

When Earle played for St. Louis of the American Association in 1890, manager Tom Loftus told reporters, "Why, Billy could 'phase' you and turn you into a horse if he got his eyes on you."

Despite their fear, his teammates were fascinated with his exhibitions of hypnotism—which he performed only on willing subjects. One person, who did not know how to swim, swam across the Ohio River after Earle hypnotized him, according to the *Cincinnati Times-Star.*

Several times, Earle put a player into a trance and made him stiff as a board. After the subject was lifted up so that his head rested on a chair and his feet on another chair, a teammate sat on him.

Earle liked to hypnotize a teammate, point to a curled-up piece of paper on the floor, and tell his subject that it was a poisonous snake. The player would

"Billy could turn you into a horse if he got his eyes on you!"

streak across the room in fright. On other occasions, Earle would stick a needle into the nose or tongue of a hypnotized player who wouldn't feel pain or even wince.

Earle also enjoyed hypnotizing a player into believing he was in a boxing match. One player "put up his dukes and fought several rounds with an old enemy," reported the *Times-Star.* "Twice he was floored and went down like a ton of coal. 'Gee, that was a soaker,' he declared as he scrambled to his feet after the last knockdown and wiped 'the blood' from his face."

The hypnotized player was then told to catch for the world's fastest pitcher. "Several 'hot ones' were tossed in and he let one or two imagined ones get away and he growled, 'Why don't you keep 'em up?' When he hurt his finger

25

there was agony depicted on his face. He threw off the glove angrily and sucked the injured member. The exhibition amused Earle as much as it did those in the audience."

Although the players laughed with Earle, they also feared him and his hypnotic powers. Whenever he entered the clubhouse, the players would maneuver awkwardly to avoid falling under his gaze. It wasn't long before they would demand that Earle be traded or released.

So in his nine-year professional career, Earle played for 13 different teams in the majors and minors even though he had a lifetime batting average of .286 in the bigs. ◊

Indians Zany Hitter Bats Upside Down

Cleveland Indians utility man Jackie Price had the strangest batting stance in major league history—he hit upside down!

The Indians' shortstop figured that since he had trouble hitting with both feet on the ground—he had a lifetime .231 average—he would try to hit upside down.

Of course, he didn't bat that way during a game. Price hit pitches while upside down during spring training in 1946. While hanging from a specially-constructed bar, Price actually could hit batting practice pitches.

Price was such a flake that he once wore a live snake around his waist like a belt. In 1947, while the Indians were on a train, he let his pet snake loose—in a crowded dining car! Seized with fright, passengers leaped from their seats in a panic to escape.

When the conductor confronted Price and demanded to know his name, the quick-thinking, fun-loving Indian answered, "Lou Boudreau, the manager." At the next stop, two policemen tried to throw the real Cleveland manager off the train. After finally convincing them he was innocent, Boudreau wanted to toss Price off the team. But club owner Bill Veeck retained Price because Veeck liked his sense of humor. ◊

JACKIE PRICE: Wacky swinger.

SUPER-SILLY
SUPERSTITIONS

Superstitions are as much a part of baseball as runs, hits, and errors. But none were more wacky than those of players from the pre-World War II days. For example:

• Al Simmons, of the Philadelphia Athletics, was in the midst of a terrible batting slump back in 1931 and tried everything to snap out of it. Nothing worked. One day, after a particularly bad batting performance, he walked out of the shower deep in thought. Then, standing nude and wet in front of his locker, he reached in and put on his hat.

The clubhouse broke up with laughter. The sight of the sopping wet, nude slugger with just a hat on was too much. But Al didn't find it funny. He quickly dressed and left the room without a word. The next day he went 4-for-4. Naturally, after the game, Al stepped from the shower, walked naked to his locker, and put on his hat. And he continued the ritual the rest of the year and batted .322.

• Hall of Fame shortstop Honus Wagner, of the Pittsburgh Pirates, believed each bat had only so many hits in it. So he discarded every bat after it collected 100 hits.

• Dizzy Trout, of the Detroit Tigers, wouldn't pitch unless he had a big red bandanna in his hip pocket.

• Cincinnati Reds manager Bill McKechnie wore the same lucky but dirty tie day in and day out during his team's successful 1940 pennant drive.

• Bobo Newsom, the most traveled hurler in the major leagues, would never tie his own shoelaces on the day he was scheduled to pitch. He'd suit up and stand in the middle of the clubhouse until somebody came over, knelt down, and laced his shoes.

• "Orator Jim" O'Rourke, of the New York Giants, got his nickname because before every big game he insisted on reciting "Hamlet's Soliloquy" to his teammates.

• Pirates first baseman Gus Suhr had a strange pregame ritual during the 1930s. He would shuffle a deck of cards, then draw one. Only number cards counted. The number he drew would dictate the number of minutes before game time that he would return to the field after batting practice.

• Before each at-bat, Chicago White Sox second baseman Eddie Collins kept a wad of gum stuck to his cap button. Whenever the count reached two strikes on him, he'd peel the gum off and pop it in his mouth. ◇

Girlie Baseball Names

Dozen of major leaguers were saddled with girlie nicknames. Among them were:

Lady Baldwin, P (1884-90)
Ginger Beaumont, OF (1899-1910)
Baby Doll Jacobson, OF (1915-27)
Little Eva Lange, OF (1893-99)
Sadie McMahon, P (1889-97)
Grandma Murphy, P (1932-47)
Tillie Shafer, INF (1909-13)

27

DIAMOND SHOCKER!!

Major Leaguers Masquerade As Women on Girls' Team

Two greats of the game started their baseball careers by dressing up as women and playing on a barnstorming team known as the Bloomer Girls.

Hall of Famer Rogers Hornsby and pitching star Smoky Joe Wood revealed that they broke into baseball by pretending to be female players.

Before World War I, the Bloomer Girls—billing themselves as the "young ladies' championship ball club of the world"—visited town after town, humbling the local men's teams.

One of the secrets to the Bloomer Girls' success was that they weren't all girls. Talented females able to play baseball and willing to leave home for a long series of one-night stands were scarce. Sometimes the ranks had to be filled by clean-shaven young men wearing wigs. Wood and Hornsby were among those masquerading as women.

"That's when I started my professional career with the Bloomer Girls," confessed Wood in the book *The Glory of Their Times.*

In 1906, at the age of 16, Wood played against the Bloomer Girls when they came to his hometown of Ness City, Kansas, and took on the local team. Wood's club beat the girls.

"After the game, the Bloomer Girls' manager asked me if I'd like to join and finish the tour with them," recalled Wood. "There were three weeks left on the trip and he offered me $20 if I'd play the infield. I thought the guy was off his rocker.

" 'Listen,' he said. 'You know as well as I do that all those Bloomer Girls aren't really girls. That third baseman's real name is Bill Compton, not Dolly Madison. And that pitcher, Lady Waddell, sure isn't [Hall of Fame pitcher Rube] Waddell's sister. If anything, he's his brother.'

" 'I figured as much,' I said. 'But your guys are wearing wigs. If you think I'm going to put on a wig, you're crazy.'

" 'No need to,' he said. 'With your baby face and longish hair you won't need one anyway.'

"So I asked my dad if I could go. He thought it was sort of unusual, but he didn't raise any objections. I guess it appealed to his sense of the absurd.

"The fact is, there were four boys on the team. In case you're wondering how the situation was in the locker room, we didn't have clubhouses in those days. We dressed in our uniforms at the hotel and rode out to the ball park from there."

Before Rogers Hornsby became one of the game's greatest second basemen, he joined the Bloomer Girls as a teenager. The small-town Texas lad figured it was the only way to see the country and get baseball experience while getting paid.

Sometimes local players got suspicious of the ringers and began tugging at the hair of all the Bloomer Girls to see whose locks would come off. A tomboy named Rosie convinced one skeptic that she was indeed a woman—one who had not only genuine hair but a nifty left hook. ◇

28

Braves play on graves of dead horses and mules

Braves Field was not just the ball park of the Boston Braves. It was also a cemetery!

From 1915 to 1952, the Braves and their opponents laid down bunts, fielded grounders, and ran bases directly over the graves of a dozen horses and mules.

The bizarre history of the field began when the team, previously known as the Beaneaters and Doves among other nicknames, was purchased in 1912 by James Gaffney, who renamed the club the Braves.

Gaffney decided the club needed a new, larger ball park. So he purchased the old Allston Golf Course on Commonwealth Avenue, just a few hundred yards from the Charles River, as the site for his new park.

During the initial construction, cave-ins occurred often. Time and again, the ground gave way and men and machinery tumbled into a muddy sink hole. Fortunately, no worker was ever killed or seriously injured.

However, there was one major cave-in that broke the hearts of animal lovers in Beantown. In 1914, while a dozen horses and mules were hauling wagons laden with dirt, the ground along what eventually became the third base line

Catcher Gets His Chicken at the Plate

Cincinnati Reds catcher Alex Trevino is upended by the San Diego Chicken who ran the bases between innings of an exhibition game with the Minnesota Twins in 1983. The chicken was called out at home.

suddenly opened into a gaping hole. Workers, wagons, and animals plunged into a 20-foot-deep chasm.

The men managed to scramble out to safety. But it was impossible to lift out the helpless horses and mules. The workers had no other choice but to shoot the animals and spare them from further misery.

The dead beasts were then covered with the dirt needed to fill up the huge sink hole.

Even after Braves Field was completed, the ball park was still plagued by small cave-ins. During one game, the area between second and third base sank eight inches, chasing Braves shortstop Rabbit Maranville to the dugout until the hole was filled in.

Over time, most everyone forgot about the sink hole and the death-dealing cave-in. But when the Braves continued to lose season after season—they finished fifth or lower 26 of the 38 years they played at Braves Field—fans began wondering if somehow the buried horses and mules were to blame.

A medium claimed she picked up a psychic message from the spirits of the dead animals which declared that the Braves would be cursed for as long as they played on the equines' graves.

Maybe there was some truth to what the medium said. In 1914, the year before moving into the new Braves Field, the club won the World Series in a four-game sweep.

But the team never copped another world championship while playing at that ball park.

It wasn't until 1957, five years after moving to Milwaukee, that the Braves won their next World Series. ◇

White Sox Apologize to Comiskey Park Ghosts

After the White Sox lost their first two games in their new stadium in 1991, two Chicago hurlers feared that ghosts from the old Comiskey Park were to blame.

The former venerable ball park—which faithfully had served as the home of the White Sox for 80 years—faced the wrecking ball after being replaced by a shiny new Comiskey Park across the street.

But in their home opener in their new digs, the White Sox were crushed 16-0 by the Toronto Blue Jays. Chicago lost again the next day, too.

To avoid an embarrassing and disastrous losing streak, Sox hurlers Jack McDowell and Scott Radinsky figured that ghosts were ticked off by the demolition of the old Comiskey Park. So the pitchers gathered rocks

...And their losing streak gets snapped

from the former park and brought them to right field of the new stadium. Then they danced around the rocks while burning one of McDowell's jerseys.

"We did it all," said McDowell. "We chanted and danced and gave a formal apology to the ghosts of old Comiskey Park."

The wacky ritual worked. The White Sox won the next three games in their new home. ◇

REVEALED!

Babe Ruth's Kinky Secret

Babe Ruth was so superstitious that he used to wear women's silk hose because he believed they warded off jinxes!

The Sultan of Swat heard that Hall of Famer Honus Wagner wore ladies' silken hose when not playing. For some crazy reason, Wagner felt that women's stockings—not men's—endowed him with a special protection from batting slumps.

It certainly seemed to work for Wagner. In his 21 years in the bigs, the Pittsburgh Pirates' shortstop batted over .300 in each of 16 seasons and finished with a lifetime average of .327.

Toward the end of Wagner's career, the Babe, who was then still a pitcher for the Boston Red Sox, learned about Wagner's bizarre superstition. Ruth wasn't about to argue with success. So the Babe, when not in uniform, chose to sport knee-length ladies' silken hose.

Whether it's coincidence or not, Ruth hit for over .300 in 17 of his 22 years in the majors and ended up with a lifetime batting average of a whopping .342.

Ruth had plenty of other quirks. When jogging in from the outfield, he always would step on second base. And on the rare occasions when he forgot to touch the bag, he would trot back out of the dugout and kick the base.

At the plate, the Babe always

BABE RUTH wore women's silk stockings when not in uniform.

knocked dirt off his cleats whenever he swung and missed a strike.

Although Ruth was a generous man, he would never loan one of his bats to a teammate. Ruth once explained, "Bats have so many hits in them, and each time I lend one to a guy and he whacks a couple of hits, all I'm doing is lopping a few points off Babe Ruth's batting average. That's why nobody uses Babe Ruth's bat—but Babe Ruth!" ◇

SUPERSTITIOUS GIANTS HIRE HUMAN GOOD LUCK CHARM

...And win 3 straight pennants!

The strangest good luck charm in baseball history was Charles "Victory" Faust—a farmer with no baseball talent who nonetheless was hired by the New York Giants because they truly believed they couldn't win without him.

Incredibly, the superstitious club actually won three straight pennants with Faust in the dugout.

Faust's story reads like a fairy tale, but it really happened. At the age of 30, the skinny, 6-foot, 2-inch Kansas farmer was told by a fortune teller that he would become the greatest pitcher the world had ever known if he joined the New York Giants.

So on July 29, 1911, Faust went to St. Louis where the Giants were playing and cornered manager John McGraw in a hotel lobby. He told McGraw what the fortune teller had said and asked for a tryout. As a lark, McGraw agreed.

Later that morning during batting practice at the ball park, Faust, dressed in his only Sunday-best suit, stepped on the mound and showed his best stuff. It was awful. All his pitches floated up to the plate at a speed so slow the catcher caught them barehanded.

McGraw then told Faust to bat and run out anything he hit. The Giants' manager signaled to his players to play a joke on Faust. When the farmer hit a weak grounder, the shortstop deliberately booted the ball. The infielders then threw the ball away while Faust—still in his Sunday suit—slid awkwardly into second, third, and home.

The players laughed themselves silly and McGraw let Faust sit on the bench for the game. The Giants lost 5-2 to the Cardinals. The next day Faust was given an ill-fitting uniform and allowed to watch the game from the dugout. This time the Giants won 8-0.

When the team left St. Louis and continued on its road trip, the players thought they had seen the last of Charlie. But by hopping freight trains, he caught up with the Giants, who were mired in a losing streak, in Boston. The surprised McGraw let Faust sit on the bench for a few days. And the Giants won every game.

The players, who were among the most superstitious in baseball, began to believe that Charlie was blessed with amazing luck that had rubbed off on them. They were also convinced Faust had other special powers, too. One day, he told catcher Chief Meyers that the Giant backstop would get a single and a double in the game. Meyers did. The next day, Faust said that the catcher would whack two singles and a homer. Incredibly, that's exactly what Meyers hit.

Now there was no doubt that Faust had to remain with the team. So McGraw, who was just as superstitious as his players, announced in August, "We're taking Charlie along to help us win the pennant."

Although Faust was never formally given a contract, the club issued him a uniform and paid his expenses. And they put him to work.

Whenever the Giants fell behind late in the game, McGraw sent Charlie to the bullpen to warm up. The manager had no intention of ever putting him in the game, but the sight of Faust in the bullpen had an astounding effect on the Giants. Almost magically, they would launch a rally and chalk up a dramatic come-from-behind victory.

By late August, the Giants had vaulted into first place. Faust, meanwhile, was getting so much attention from the press and fans that he signed a $200 a week vaudeville contract. But in his first week away from the team, the Giants lost three games and dropped out of first—so he broke his showbiz contract and returned to the team.

Sure enough, the Giants started winning again and they captured the pennant—their first in six years—by 7½ games.

Out of gratitude, McGraw actually let Faust pitch briefly once the Giants had clinched the pennant. Charlie appeared in two games in 1911, giving up a total of two hits and two runs in two innings.

Faust's luck first showed signs of faltering when, despite his prediction of a world championship for New York, the Giants lost the World Series to the Philadelphia A's.

The faith his followers had in him was shaken. In fact, McGraw refused to give Faust his uniform back in 1912, although he was allowed to stay with the team and sit on the bench. The

A Boatload of Batty Braves

Two loyal Braves rooters brought this canoe from Gardner, Mass., to Boston to observe Gardner Day at Braves Field. Three of the tribe, led by tom-tom thumping chief Billy Southworth, entertain the fans before the start of the game with the Cards in 1948. Trying to paddle across the infield are (from left) Earl Torgeson, Bob Elliott and Tommy Holmes.

Giants won the pennant again. But, like the year before, New York lost the World Series.

In 1913, Charlie's luck was running out. Although he still had many believers on the team, others were beginning to think of him as a nuisance. Nevertheless, the Giants won their third straight pennant. But they lost their third straight World Series.

The Giants dumped Faust for good. When he left, so did their fortunes. Over the next three years, the team tumbled to second, eighth (last place), and fourth.

Faust, meanwhile, was confined to a mental hospital shortly after leaving the club and died in 1915 of tuberculosis.

Still, he came closer to fulfilling the fortune teller's prophecy than anyone could have imagined. Charlie "Victory" Faust actually pitched in the major leagues . . . and, in a weird way, helped the Giants win three straight pennants. ◇

The *Craziest*
Names in Baseball History!

Baseball players have had some of the zaniest nicknames in all of sports. Among the more outrageous monikers are:

Chicken Hawks, 1B, 1921, 1925
Eyechart Gwosdz, C, 1981-84
Hippity Hopp, 1B, 1939-52
Ding Dong Bell, P, 1952, 1955
Leaky Fausett, 3B, 1944
Sting Ray, P, 1965-74
Pickles Gerken, OF, 1927-28
Deedle Moran, OF, 1912
Zaza Harvey, OF, 1900-02
Ubbo Ubbo Hornung, OF, 1879-90
Puddin' Head Jones, 3B, 1947-61
Peek-A-Boo Veech, INF, 1884-90
Lollipop Killefer, OF, 1907-16
Prunes Moolic, C, 1886

Swamp Baby Wilson, SS, 1931-35
Hill Billy Bildilli, P, 1937-41
Sweetbreads Bailey, P, 1919-21
Pig House, C, 1950-61
Porky Pawelek, C, 1946
Horse Belly Sargent, INF, 1921
Earache Meyer, OF, 1913-25
Dimples Lott, OF, 1903
Bootnose Hofmann, C, 1919-28
Schnozz Lombardi, C, 1931-47
Bitsy Mott, SS, 1945
Beauty McGowan, OF, 1922-37
Piano Legs Hickman, INF, 1897-1908
Poodles Hutcheson, OF, 1933
Meow Gilmore, P, 1944
Kangaroo Jones, OF, 1901-15
Grasshopper Lillie, OF, 1883-86
Mongoose Lukon, OF, 1941-47

★★★

There's a secret message on the green monster—the left-field fence at Fenway Park, home of the Boston Red Sox. Marked vertically on the scoreboard face are the Morse Code initials of deceased former Red Sox owner Thomas Yawkey and his wife Jean.

DARRELL EVANS:

How a UFO saved my career

Slugger Darrell Evans revealed that a close encounter with a UFO helped give his sagging career new life.

Evans, an All-Star power hitter with the Atlanta Braves and San Francisco Giants throughout the 1970s, was beginning to slow down by 1982. At the time, the 35-year-old Giants' third baseman was wondering if he was near the end of his remarkable career.

Then in June he and his wife Ladonna experienced a sight that changed their lives—they saw a UFO.

The couple was sitting outside their Pleasanton, California, home when they spotted a strange light in the night sky. "The closer it got, the brighter it got," Evans told reporters later. "What made it so unusual was that it was moving so slowly. And there was no sound whatsoever.

DARRELL EVANS: Amazed by UFO.

"It ended up stopping about 60 yards from our house and just hovered there, almost over a neighbor's house. The thing was a triangular shape, with the back flattened out. The front had a rounded nose and some sort of dome. A glow was coming from the back. It was about 20 to 30 yards wide, maybe 15 yards from the nose to the flat back end and was a dull gray color."

He and his wife looked at each other in stunned amazement and neither said a word. They watched in silence for about a minute before Evans decided to get his camera. "All of a sudden, without any sound, it took off like a jet and was gone," he said.

The UFO had a profound effect on him, Evans said. It made him think about the larger events in life, and his personal problems seemed less significant.

"At the time of the sighting, I was sitting on the bench for the first time in my career. The UFO gave me a more positive outlook.

"When I got a chance to play again, I approached things a lot more intensely than before."

Evans walloped five home runs the first month after seeing the UFO. The next season he hit 30 round-trippers and drove in 82 runs for his best season in 10 years. Evans then joined the Detroit Tigers and led the American League in homers in 1985 with 40. A career that was on the skids soared to new heights—thanks to an encounter with a UFO. ◇

35

Houston Hires Witch Doctor To Rid Team of Losing Jinx

When an expansion team found itself in danger of setting an all-time record for futility, it turned to a witch doctor for help.

WITCH DOCTOR hexes the Phils.

In 1962, their first year in existence, the Houston Colt .45s were desperate. They were on their way to becoming the first team ever to lose an entire season series to an opposing club.

While many teams had lost all but one game to the same club in a season, none had ever lost every game. When the Colt .45s (forerunners of the Astros) lost their first 15 games against the Philadelphia Phillies, the new club was in a good position to set a team record in ignobility.

For its final three-game homestand with the Phillies, which included a doubleheader, the Houston management publicized the bad news record and scheduled a "Break the Jinx Night" for the twinbill. Then the front office hired Dr. Mesabubu, a ficticious witch doctor from the Wauwautuau tribe, to hex the Phillies.

Shortly before the game, the witch doctor—decked out in head dress and skins—performed a ceremonial dance in front of the Philadelphia dugout that freaked out a couple of Phillies who were strong believers in the occult. They refused to leave the bench until the witch doctor left the field.

As a backup to the shaman, the Houston front office brought in Joe Bftstlk—the human version of the bad-luck-attracting character in the "L'il Abner" comic strip. Joe went out to the bullpen and put a double whammy on Phillies pitcher Art Mahaffey during his pregame warmup.

Then, as extra insurance, Colt .45 fans were given half off the ticket price if they brought jinx-breakers to the ball park. Thousands of fans brought four-leaf clovers, rabbits' feet, horseshoes, lucky old shoes, and black cats. One fan even brought a skunk.

The efforts of the crowd, Joe Bftstlk, and Dr. Mesabubu certainly had a tremendous impact—on the Colt .45s.

They dropped both games, 3-2 and 5-3, making their record an embarrasing 0-17 against Philly with just one game left.

The next day, without the benefit of supernaturalism, Houston avoided humiliation by beating the Phillies—and the jinx—4-1. ◇

'Curse of Ex-Cubs' Dooms World Series Favorites

No baseball curse is more real ... more powerful ... more terrifying than the Curse of the Ex-Cubs. The hex causes any team with three or more former Chicago Cubs on its roster to lose the World Series.

Since 1946—the year after the Cubs last won a pennant—14 teams have gone into the World Series with at least three ex-Cubs—and 13 have lost. The only club to defy the curse was the Pittsburgh Pirates in the 1960 World Series. Somehow they managed to beat the New York Yankees four games to three despite being outscored (55-27), outhit (91-60), and outpitched (3.54 ERA to 7.11).

No more powerful example of the ex-Cub curse can be found than the plight that befell the 1990 Oakland A's. With the year's best record (103-59), the A's were overwhelming favorites to whip the Cincinnati Reds (91-71) in the Series. Oakland, which had breezed to the world championship the year before, was called by many the best team in the history of baseball.

But there was one major difference between the champion A's of 1989 and the 1990 squad—they had added another ex-Cub. "They had the arrogance to defy the ex-Cub factor," said Ron Berler, a Chicago teacher and baseball fan who discovered the curse in 1981. "In 1989, the A's had only two ex-Cubs, so they were safe. But they couldn't leave well enough alone. They

went out and got Scott Sanderson, a pitcher they didn't need, and he became the fatal third ex-Cub."

Berler believes that all ex-Cubs carry a debilitating virus he calls "Cubness." And when three of them are on the same team, the virus spreads to the whole club. But the only symptom—losing—doesn't appear until the team reaches that hallowed plateau which the Cubs haven't found in nearly half a century—the World Series.

When Berler publicly warned that the A's were doomed, the experts scoffed at him, declaring that mighty Oakland would disprove such nonsense.

So what happened? The Reds—with only two former Cubs on their roster—stunned the baseball world by routing the A's in four straight games.

"This was the greatest challenge the ex-Cub factor ever faced," said Berler. "Intuitively, the factor itself knew it was being challenged.

"So what did it do? It humiliated this A's team as no team has been humiliated in baseball history.

"Who can doubt it anymore?" ◇

37

Fear of Flying Grounds MVP's Career

At the height of his career, Boston Red Sox star Jackie Jensen quit baseball—because he was gripped by an uncontrollable fear of flying.

From 1954-59, the power-hitting outfielder had driven in more runs—at least 97 a season—than anyone in the American League, including Ted Williams and Mickey Mantle. In 1958, Jensen was named the league's Most Valuable Player. The following year, he belted 28 homers and led the league in RBI with 112.

Then Jensen shocked the baseball world. The slugger who could overcome a pitcher's best stuff couldn't overcome a flying phobia and was forced to retire.

"I don't know when it started or why or how," he told reporters. "It's just there. I don't have any other fears, just that one."

Early in his career, teams generally traveled by train. But as clubs gradually switched to planes, Jensen frantically tried to cope with the change. He avoided flying whenever possible. While the rest of his team flew, he rode trains. And he once drove 800 miles from Boston to Detroit just to avoid a flight.

When he simply had to fly, his Red Sox teammates pumped him full of sleeping pills just before a flight. "I would be out when they put me in my seat," said Jensen. "Then when the engines started, I'd be wide awake and everybody else on the plane would be fast asleep."

In desperation, Jensen sought the help of psychiatrists and even a hypnotist. But nothing worked and he

JACKIE JENSEN: Safer on land.

announced his retirement at the young age of 32.

After sitting out the 1960 season, Jensen attempted a comeback with the Red Sox who needed him because Ted Williams had retired. But during the first month of the season, Jensen bolted the team moments before it was scheduled to fly to Kansas City. He rejoined the Red Sox ten days later.

The club had handled his phobia with kid gloves up to this point. But later in the season, Boston withheld his pay for games missed because he would not fly with the team. In 1961, he played well below his usual standards, hitting only 13 homers and driving in 66 runs.

This time, Jensen quit for good—a brilliant career grounded by the fear of flying. ◇

Baseball's Wackiest Superstition

...Cleveland outfielder had to touch others last!

Superstition was literally a touchy subject for Cleveland Indians reserve outfielder Kevin Rhomberg.

Rhomberg, who played from 1982-84, believed that if anyone touched him, he had to touch that person back—an idiosyncracy that made him a favorite target for practical jokes.

"He wouldn't let anyone touch him last," said Milt Thompson, who played against Rhomberg in winter ball. "One time, I took a baseball and touched him with it and then threw it over the fence. He went out there and tried to find it. Sometimes his teammates would gang up on him and they'd all touch him at the same time and then run in different directions. He'd go crazy trying to touch them all back."

During a winter game in Venezuela, Rhomberg was at bat when Danny Rohn of the Chicago Cubs ran up behind him, touched him on the back, and dashed off. "I was going to chase him into the dugout, but I'd have been mugged," Rhomberg recalled.

But Rhomberg had a plan. He was staying at the same hotel as Rohn. So Kevin got up at 3:30 a.m. and knocked on Rohn's door. When the sleepy player opened it, Kevin touched Rohn's hand and ran off.

As word spread about his weird superstition, "it seemed like half the American League tried to touch him," said former teammate Rick Manning. "The fans got into the act, too. They sent Rhomberg letters saying, 'You touched my letter—I got you last.' So he'd write back so he could be last."

Asked to explain his superstition, Kevin said, "I don't know why I do it. I've been doing it since I was a kid."

Rhomberg had another bizarre idiosyncracy—he would never turn to his right. If he stepped off the team bus and was supposed to turn right, Rhomberg made a complete left turn first before proceeding.

His no-right-turn superstition affected the way he played baseball. "If he approached home plate from the right side, he'd walk in front of the plate and make a left to the batter's box," recalled Manning. "If he made an out at first, he'd always turn left 270 degrees before going into the first-base dugout.

"He was the most superstitious player I've ever seen." ◇

KEVIN RHOMBERG: Touch and go!

Yankee Star's *Gnawing* Habit —He Chews Bats

...And ends up with a splinter in his tongue!

New York Yankees first baseman Hal Chase had one of baseball's weirdest habits—he chewed on bats!

And it led to one of baseball's weirdest injuries. A doctor had to be summoned to remove a splinter from Chase's tongue.

Chase, who played for the Yankees from 1905 to 1912, had an inexplicable craving for wood. He would simply pick up a bat—any bat—and chew on the handle. Teammates figured he bit bats because he wanted to test the quality of the wood. Others said he enjoyed the taste of the lumber. Chase himself never explained why he did it.

It looked like his days of bat-biting might end when he chewed on a handle and wound up with a painful sliver in his tongue. The splinter was embedded so deeply that the chagrined player needed a doctor to extract it.

When New York sportswriters heard the story, they were skeptical at first, until one of them confronted the team bat boy. "Yes sir, it's true," said the bat boy. "Almost every bat we have around our bench has got Mr. Chase's

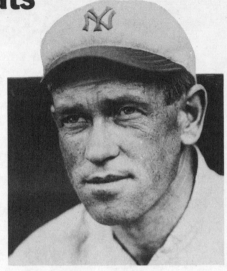

HAL CHASE didn't knock on wood, he nibbled on it!

teeth marks on it. He just sorta gnaws on them."

"Can he tell anything about a bat by biting it?" the sportswriter asked.

"Mr. Chase never lets anybody know what he finds out by biting the bat," said the bat boy.

Whatever it was that compelled Chase to bite bats was apparently pretty powerful. He continued chewing on bats long after he had the splinter removed from his tongue. ◇

Wild Pitch Lands in Ump's Pocket!

Philadelphia Phillies catcher Mike Ryan went crazy looking for a wild pitch—until the umpire pulled it out of his pocket.

During a 1970 spring training game against the St. Louis Cardinals, Phillies hurler Ken Reynolds delivered a fast ball that hit home plate, bounced up, and skipped off Ryan's shoulder. Ryan frantically scrambled all around the plate looking for the ball, but there was no sign of it. Meanwhile, the runner on first scampered to second.

Home plate umpire Jerry Dale then called time. He fished the wild pitch out of his right coat pocket and handed the ball to Ryan with a big grin.

Fastest 9-Inning Game in History — Only 31 Minutes!

...And Other Stories of Unbelievable Games

Arctic Leaguers Play *Brrr*-Ball in 50-Degree-Below-Zero Weather!

In the hardiest league in baseball history, sailors from seven whaling ships iced in for the winter in the Arctic Circle played the national pastime to brighten their long dreary months of frigid isolation.

Never has baseball been played under such horrendous conditions. The diamond was laid out on a bleak chunk of ice. Temperature at game time was often 50 degrees below zero. Blizzards made it impossible for fielders to see the ball or for runners to find the bases.

But despite the harsh weather, the games went on—because league rules prohibited postponements!

Brrr-ball was played during the winter of 1893-94 in a harbor near the mouth of Alaska's MacKenzie River, just 20 degrees south of the North Pole. Seven whaling ships from San Francisco—the Balaena, Grampus, Mary D. Hume, Newport, Narwhal, Jeanette, and Karluck—were iced in for a nine-month winter.

When a crewman discovered a crate of bats and balls in the hold of one of the ships, the sailors formed a league of seven teams—one of seamen, another of cooks and waiters, a third of officers, and four other squads. The teams—the Hoodlums, Walruses, Roaring Gimlets, Auroras, Pig-Stickers, Blubbers, and Invincibles—vied for a piece of canvas nailed to a broom handle and dubbed, "The Arctic Whaleman's Pennant."

Team representatives drew up a set of rules and a schedule and agreed that each game would be played "regardless of the weather."

The teams had one month of "spring training" before the league began play in December. On Opening Day, in relatively balmy 38-degree-below-zero weather, the Roaring Gimlets routed the Pig-Stickers 62-49.

The wild score was a harbinger of things to come. Racking up over a combined 100 runs a game was common even though most contests were called after four innings because darkness fell so quickly.

There were often more errors than hits because of the field of ice, weather conditions, and the fact that the players dressed in Eskimo garb and wore fur mittens instead of baseball gloves. The league's defensive star, a roly-poly Scotsman, stopped hot grounders by lying down in front of them.

At first, any ground ball was a potential home run if it got past the infield because it would roll for several hundred yards on the ice. But eventually the men erected snow bank fences to hold grounders to doubles and triples.

Baserunning was a real adventure. It was difficult to get up momentum on the slick ice. But once the runner got up to speed, he had to begin his slide 30 feet from the base or risk sliding past it.

Even in this remote corner of the world, baseball attracted fans. Games were attended by dozens of enthusiastic Kogmulliks Eskimos, who sometimes got carried away. Early in the season, they often rushed onto the diamond whenever a ball was hit and held the baserunner until the fielder had a chance to retrieve the ball.

Unfortunately, no written record has been found revealing what team won the first and only Arctic Whalemen's Pennant. ◇

Long-Haired, Bearded Barnstormers...

House of David: Baseball's Original Hippy Team

The House of David wowed fans as the most outrageous team in baseball history—because its players sported long beards and braided hair and lived in a commune.

From 1910-1941, these shaggy, whiskered wizards barnstormed across the country, challenging local teams—and coming away winners most of the time.

The House of David team was founded by Benjamin Purnell, who claimed that in 1903 a white dove had alighted on his shoulder and told him he was the sixth son of the House of David. Purnell then established a self-sustaining commune in Benton Harbor, Michigan, that attracted

thousands of faithful followers.

All who joined the sect had to cede their property and cash to the common fund. With the money, Purnell established stores, hotels, an amusement park, a concert band—and a traveling baseball team.

In 1923, Purnell was accused of having so many illicit affairs with young women that he was ousted from the sect. His wife Mary took over the team and hired the best players available whether or not they were members of the order. But all players were required to wear long hair and beards—the trademark of the sect.

The House of David actually had three teams, each playing about 200 games per season and winning about 150. Many times the Davids played both Saturday and Sunday doubleheaders and sometimes triple-headers.

The Davids loved to keep the crowd in stitches. Their favorite play was the hidden ball trick. One of the players would produce the ball from beneath his long beard and put the tag on a startled baserunner. The team enjoyed pulling off wacky triple steals in which three runners would end up on the same base before two of them then would scamper off safely to other bases.

But the main attraction for fans was the Davids' pregame warmup act. Five players stood in a line about 15 feet from a batter who bunted the ball to one of the fielders. The player snared the ball, brought it back through his legs, around his back, and then tossed it to another player who did the same thing. The ball weaved its way over, under, and around the players' bodies while another ball was hit to them. As the tempo increased, balls, bats, and gloves went weaving through the line of players at the same time.

Besides being entertainers, the Davids were darn good players—equal to those on a AAA minor league team. During spring training in 1933, the House of David beat the Philadelphia A's 9-7 and the St. Louis Browns 1-0. Davids hurler Sig Jakucki, who shut out St. Louis, so impressed the Browns that they later signed him up. Several major leaguers ended their baseball careers playing for the Davids. The most famous of all was Hall of Fame pitcher Grover Cleveland Alexander. Goober Dean—the younger brother of Dizzy and Daffy Dean—also pitched for the Davids.

By the late 1930s, the Davids began to decline in popularity and in talent. As the minor league teams began snapping up young prospects, the House of David had to fill the roster with has-beens and never-will-be's.

Before long, baseball's first hippy team became a faded memory. Hair today, gone tomorrow. ◇

Buzzing Bee Gives Babe Honey of a Homer!

Babe Ruth would have hit 713 lifetime homers instead of 714 if it hadn't been for a bothersome bee.

In a 1921 game between the Philadelphia Athletics and the New York Yankees, Ruth stepped to the plate against A's hurler Slim Harriss, who was suddenly getting harassed by a dive-bombing bee. The pitcher tried to brush the annoying insect away as it buzzed around his head.

Finally, Harriss decided to ignore the bee and went into his windup. Just as the hurler was about to release the ball, the bee stung him in the back of the neck. Harriss yelped in pain and tried to hold up on his follow-through. But the ball slipped from his hand and floated lazily up to the plate.

Ruth couldn't believe his eyes—the pitch looked easier to hit than a batting practice toss. With one powerful swing, the Babe launched the ball high into the right field bleachers for a four-bagger.

Said Ruth after the game, "I give full credit for my homer today to that busy little bee out on the mound." ◇

Expos, Padres Play On After Lights Blow Out

When the stadium lights failed, the Montreal Expos and the visiting San Diego Padres still tried to out-do each other—by performing comedy skits!

On June 6, 1978, the Expos held a 2-0 lead in the bottom of the sixth when the lights unexpectedly went out at Montreal's Olympic Stadium. The park was plunged into darkness because of a blowout in a nearby station. But after 20 minutes, the lights on one side of the stadium came on. The other side flickered briefly, then went out.

With the game delayed by unacceptably dim light, the teams decided to play like they never had before.

San Diego's Derrel Thomas tried to throw a ball out of the stadium because no one had ever hit one out. After failing in several attempts, Thomas rolled balls down the third base line. To the crowd's delight, he mimicked an umpire signaling whether the ball had rolled fair or foul.

Umpire Bruce Froemming then hustled onto the field and waved Thomas aside. The ump took a ball at home plate and rolled it right on the line all the way down to first base. When Thomas tried to copy him, a bucketful of baseballs was flung from the Padres' dugout. So Thomas tried kicking the balls back into the dugout. The fans booed whenever he whiffed on a kick.

Not to be outdone, the Expos ran out and put on an infield drill—without a ball. Each player pantomimed the motions, making spectacular phantom catches and phantom throws while the crowd roared with laughter.

Next, Padres shortstop Ozzie Smith strolled to home plate and did two cartwheels and a backward flip. The Expos countered with Warren Cromartie, who promptly fell flat on his face—deliberately—while trying to imitate Smith.

Then Thomas and Expo Andre Dawson staged a footrace from the dugout to second base, with Dawson winning easily.

The Expos put on an infield drill—without a ball

Next, Padres pitcher Gaylord Perry, long infamous for accusations that he doctored the ball, came out to the mound with a bucket filled with a greasy substance. The Padres' Randy Jones stepped into the batter's box.

Then umpire Billy Williams rushed out to the mound and staged an elaborate search of Perry, looking for a foreign substance. Satisfied, he turned his back and walked away. Perry promptly dunked the ball into the bucket of greasy stuff—and dazzled the crowd with some of the biggest-breaking curve balls ever seen.

By now the delay had reached 69 minutes and still the lights weren't fixed. But most of the crowd of 13,702 had stayed to enjoy the show. Finally, officials suspended the game (the Expos won the continuation, 4-0, the next night).

Of the teams' zany actions, umpire Froemming said, "There's nothing wrong with having a little fun at a time like this." ◇

Majors' Most Evenly-Matched Ball Game!

The Pittsburgh Pirates and Brooklyn Dodgers played nine innings of almost mirror-image baseball in the most incredible tie game of all time.

On Aug. 13, 1910, at Brooklyn's Washington Park, the two clubs played to an 8-8 tie when the game was called by darkness after nine innings. What set this contest apart from all the others were the statistics, showing it was the most evenly-matched game in baseball history. Here's the unbelievable final score for the game:

	AB	R	H	PO	A	E
Pittsburgh	38	8	13	27	12	2
Brooklyn	38	8	13	27	12	2

But that's not all. The clubs were identical in many other ways, too. Each team used ten players, including two pitchers. Each team recorded five strikeouts and three walks. Each team had one hit batsman.

Each catcher was charged with a passed ball, recorded six putouts and one assist, and also batted four times with one hit.

Each second baseman banged out two hits and scored two runs. Each shortstop collected two hits. Each right fielder had two hits, five at-bats, and one putout. Each center fielder had five at-bats and two putouts.

And each first baseman had four at-bats and scored one run. ◇

Lightweights Crush Heavyweights

In the first game ever pitting a team of players who were each over 200 pounds against a squad of men who were each under 150 pounds, the lightweights pounded the heavyweights 46-16.

The two unnamed teams, made up of members of the Commercial Exchange, played their wacky game at Recreation Park in Philadelphia on May 24, 1883.

The teams "afforded some display of science and a great deal of amusement to a large crowd of ladies and gentlemen," said *The Philadelphia Press,* which covered the game. "The stout gentlemen were rather too much for their [thin] opponents so far as solid work is concerned, but when it came to running . . . the lightweights kicked gravel in a way that called out torrents of applause."

The lightweights ran the heavyweights ragged and chalked up an incredible 18 runs in the first inning. At the end of the second frame, the score was 23-3. The quicker, faster lightweights banged out 56 hits to the

...Pound out 46-16 win

heavyweights' 20 and breezed to an amazingly easy seven-inning victory.

The game wasn't decided so much by the hitting as by the fielding—or, more accurately, the lack of it. Unbelievably, according to the box score, the lightweights scored just seven earned runs while the heavyweights tallied only three.

The heavyweights sought revenge in a September game that drew so much interest schools let out early, shops closed, and even court was adjourned. A specially-erected grandstand was completely full.

This time, the heavyweights were not about to be bullied by the lightweights. The heavyweights won 22-20. ◇

Game Called—On Account of Grasshoppers

Like a scene out of Alfred Hitchcock's *"The Birds,"* tens of thousands of huge grasshoppers swarmed over a Texas League ball park, harassing players and fans and forcing the postponement of the game.

The bizarre blizzard of bugs interrupted play in the first inning of the second game of a 1972 twilight doubleheader between the visiting Amarillo Giants and the Midland Cubs.

"The whole park was under grasshoppers," said Giants manager Denny Sommers. "The grasshoppers were so bad that they were dimming the lights. I was reluctant to talk because I was afraid I might eat one.

They were all over my mouth and everywhere."

When the hoppers hit the stadium, fans started screaming and flailing away at the insects to no avail. "The bugs were all over people," recalled Giants infielder Glenn Stitzel. "They were getting in ladies' hair and everything."

The horde of three-inch grasshoppers covered the field and blanketed the air, making it tough for batters and fielders. One long drive that normally would have gone over

Buggy Ball Game

Groundskeepers wave flaming papers and shoot insect guns at a swarm of gnats which drove Baltimore Orioles pitcher Hoyt Wilhelm from the mound during a game with the Chicago White Sox in 1959.

the fence stayed in the park for an out because it had hit so many bugs on its flight.

"You could hear the ball hitting grasshoppers as the pitch came in," said the Cubs' Pete LaCock, who was at bat when the game was called. "There were marks from dead grasshoppers all over the ball. If you hit a popup, grasshoppers would fall out of the sky."

Meanwhile, in the bullpen, players were swinging bats at the bugs. "I hit three taters [long drives]—it's the best wood I've had all year," declared Giants relief pitcher Lee White. "I couldn't believe how many there were. It was like a scene out of the Bible."

Fellow relief pitcher Hal Jeffcoat had a ready explanation for the grasshopper invasion. "[Teammate] Randy Cohen was doing a rain dance, but he used the wrong words and the grasshoppers came instead." ◇

Indians Use Army Tank To Steal Catcher's Signs

Some teams will do anything to win a game, but the 1955 Cleveland Indians set a new standard in chicanery. They resorted to using an Army tank to steal the signs of the Kansas City Athletics' catcher.

"We were playing a doubleheader on Armed Forces Day," recalled Indians left fielder Ralph Kiner. "The Army put on a big show between games. They rolled out tanks and all sorts of equipment, and drove them around the edge of the field. Then, before the second game started, they parked their equipment in an area behind the outfield fence."

A few yards away, in the bullpen, Indians pitcher Hal Newhouser noticed a rangefinder on one of the tanks. He slyly climbed into the tank and began focusing the rangefinder on home plate.

"He keyed in on the Kansas City catcher [Joe Astroth], big as life," said Kiner. "There were the signs, staring Hal in the face. He called them out and somebody else got on the bullpen phone and alerted our dugout who passed them on to our batters."

The Indians scored in the first five innings en route to a 9-2 drubbing of the A's.

"We were bombing the hell out of the Kansas City pitchers right from the start of the game. [A's manager] Lou Boudreau knew we were getting the pitches from some place, but he couldn't figure it out. He went nuts trying to find out, but never did." ◇

Mets Get Surprise Early Shower

The New York Mets went to the showers early in a 1988 exhibition game at the team's new spring training complex in Port St. Lucie, Florida.

The visiting Los Angeles Dodgers were at bat in the eighth inning when 37 outfield sprinklers suddenly erupted in unison, forcing the Mets to flee.

The wet 'n' wild game had to be stopped for about five minutes until the poorly-timed watering system was shut down.

Fastest 9-Inning Game In History—31 Minutes!

In the fastest professional baseball game ever played, two teams from the North Carolina League whizzed through their nine-inning contest in a breathtaking 31 minutes!

Shortly before the visiting Winston-Salem Twins were to meet the Asheville Tourists in the last week of the 1916 season, Twins skipper Charles Clancy asked a favor of Tourists player-manager Jack Corbett. "The last train for Winston-Salem leaves at 3 o'clock this afternoon," said Clancy. "Can you help us out?"

Corbett agreed to move the game's starting time from 2 p.m. to 1:28 p.m. and promised that his team would speed up the game. Then came a brainstorm. Since neither club was in the pennant race and the game was otherwise meaningless, why not try to break the record for the fastest game? Back then the 1910 contest between Atlanta and Mobile of the Southern Association had been the fastest game played—in a stunning 32 minutes.

In the Twins-Tourists game, every batter swung at the first pitch—which in every case was lobbed right down the middle. If the batter got a hit, he kept running to the next base until he was tagged out. (Three runners avoided getting tagged.)

No sooner was the last out made in an inning, then both teams were racing to change sides. Sometimes pitches were delivered before the fielders were even in position.

In the third inning, Asheville hurler Doc Lowe pitched before his catcher arrived and the batter singled to center field. When the throw from the outfield came in wild and headed toward the Winston-Salem dugout, Twins on-deck hitter Frank Nesser grabbed the ball and threw out his own teammate at second base.

The game was such a travesty that Tourists owner L.L. Jenkins, who made a habit of buying his own ticket, asked for a refund, which was granted. He offered refunds to anyone else who wanted them, but there were few takers because this "meaningless" game suddenly had taken on some rather wacky historical significance.

At 1:59 p.m.—just as several unsuspecting fans were arriving expecting to watch a game—the final out was made. The nine-inning contest, which the Twins won 2-1, had been played in record time, beating the old mark by one minute.

Winston-Salem had no trouble making its train.

Interestingly, one of the fans at the game was 15-year-old Thomas Wolfe of Asheville. Years later, as one of America's great novelists, Wolfe based some of his characters in *Look Homeward, Angel* and *You Can't Go Home Again* on the players in the game. ◇

★★★

He Had the Pitcher's Number

When Hank Aaron of the Atlanta Braves hit his 715th home run to break Babe Ruth's record, he was wearing No. 44—the same number as opposing pitcher Al Downing of the Los Angeles Dodgers.

One-Legged Players vs. One-Armed Men

In the most amazing and inspirational baseball game ever played, a team of one-armed players competed against a club of one-legged men!

This unbelievable scene unfolded on May 23, 1883, at Recreation Park in Philadelphia where a group of determined men wanted to prove that even though they were disabled, they could still play baseball. The Snorkey Baseball Club—made up of those who had lost an arm in work-related accidents or during the Battle of Gettysburg—had challenged the Hoppers, a team whose players worked for the Reading Railroad and had each lost a leg in a railroad accident.

Some of the best action happened even before the first pitch was thrown. Hundreds of spectators—many of whom were disabled themselves—waged spirited bets over the outcome of the game. The gamblers made the Hoppers 5-4 favorites, figuring that the one-armed Snorkeys would have a tough time not only hitting for power but catching the balls off the bats of the hard-hitting Hoppers.

"Half of the goodly crowd of spectators were either one-armed or had stub legs," *The Philadelphia Press* reported. "Many of them were scarred veterans of war, some had been run over by the [railroad] cars, others had their arms sawed off or their legs struck by lightning. A more melancholy, battered-up set of men were never gotten together."

It was a cold, drizzly day and the diamond was muddy, but the crowd

ONE-ARMED PETE GRAY amazed the baseball world as an outfielder for the St. Louis Browns in 1945. After fielding the ball, Gray would toss it up in the air and drop his glove in one motion, then catch the ball with his left hand, and fire it back to the infield.

and players were psyched up for this history-making game. According to the *Press,* "The Hoppers looked very attractive in white undershirts, with their legs done up in slings, and the Snorkeys elicited much enthusiasm by appearing in equally white undershirts with arms strapped to their shoulder blades . . . Some were wrapped in leather, others with flannel, some with canvas, and some with calico or white muslin."

In the top of the first inning, George Dowd, playing with an artificial wooden leg, led off for the Hoppers and singled to center. The next batter, Morris Haines, swatted a grounder to the shortstop. Haines would have beaten the throw to first if only his peg leg hadn't got stuck in the mud halfway up the baseline. Nevertheless, the Hoppers—some gamely hobbling around the bases on crutches—amazed the crowd by scoring four runs in the inning.

Just as astounding, the Snorkeys struck back quickly to tie the score in their half of the frame. Despite swinging with only one arm, the Snorkeys displayed remarkable hitting power and kept piling on the runs in each succeeding inning. The Snorkeys showed little mercy and took full advantage of their opponents' handicap. Because the Hopper outfielders played on crutches and were unable to cover much ground, fly balls fell for doubles. Infielders with peg legs had little mobility, thus allowing easy grounders to bounce through the diamond for singles. Time and again, Hopper fielders, much to their dismay, would chase balls only to be stopped when their peg legs or crutches sank in the soft turf or mud.

Only George Dowd, with a well-oiled artificial leg that bent at the knee, had no problem with his handicap. Dowd "could run like a streak and the Snorkeys gave up trying to put him out in disgust," said the *Press.*

But Dowd couldn't carry the team by himself. When the game was called after five innings because of rain, many bettors were disappointed—the Snorkeys had trounced the Hoppers 34-11. But in reality, both sides proved they were winners. ◇

Braves Lose 8 Home Games —In 4 Days!

Boston had the home field *disadvantage* in September, 1928. The Braves played four straight doubleheaders in Beantown with the New York Giants—and lost every game.

The daily double dose of defeat began when Boston was routed 4-1 and 11-0 by New York. The next day the Braves lost to the Giants 11-6 and 7-6.

New York then drubbed Boston again in their third straight twinbill, 12-2 and 7-6. The following day, the Braves were whipped twice, 6-2 and 5-1, for their eighth consecutive loss in four days at the hands of the New Yorkers.

After the eight-game, four-day homestand, the only thing that made the Braves happy was seeing the Giants leave town.

Boston's string of doubleheaders was part of a grueling quirk in the schedule. Incredibly, because of makeup games from rainouts, the Braves were forced to play nine consecutive twinbills in September. They split four double dips and were swept in five. ◇

Outfielder Catches Ball Underwater...
Pirates and Dodgers Play Game in Knee-Deep Flood

In the only game where outfielders could have used life vests, the Pittsburgh Pirates and Brooklyn Dodgers played a bizarre doubleheader on a field that was under as much as three feet of water.

In 1902, heavy rains had caused the Allegheny River to spill over its banks. As the water crept closer and closer to the Pirates' ball park, Exposition Park, storm sewers backed up, which caused massive flooding of the field.

Normally, club officials would have cancelled the twinbill. But it was July 4th and first-place Pittsburgh was slated to play second-place Brooklyn in a morning-afternoon doubleheader that was expected to draw a big holiday crowd.

So when more than 10,000 fans showed up for the first game, it went on as scheduled even though the flood waters were more than a foot deep in the outfield and rising. Because of the flood, the umpires made a new ground rule. Any ball hit into the outfield water would be a single, no matter where it landed.

In the morning game, Brooklyn won 3-0 as both teams had suprisingly little trouble with the underwater outfield.

But the afternoon game was a different story. By then, the flood waters had moved to within 20 feet of second base (the position, ironically, of Brooklyn's Tim Flood). Meanwhile, the outfielders were forced to slosh around in knee-deep water. The only balls they could catch were flies hit almost directly at them.

As luck would have it, the Brooklyn right fielder was 5-foot, 4-inch "Wee Willie" Keeler, whose short stature made plowing through the outfield flood particularly difficult. As a result,

several balls that normally would have been easy outs plopped into the water for Pirate base hits.

Pittsburgh outfielders had it much easier. Because Pirates pitcher Jack Chesbro had a great sinker ball, the Dodgers' batters kept hitting ground balls to the infielders all afternoon.

The two teams hurriedly played the game before the water completely engulfed the infield. Batboys used towels to dry off the baseball every time it was hit.

Pittsburgh was winning 4-0 in the top of the ninth when the Dodgers launched a rally. With two on and two out, Brooklyn shortstop Bill Dahlen blasted the ball high and deep. Pirates left fielder Ginger Beaumont half swam, half waded for the ball before making a desperate lunge. He snared the ball as he disappeared in a big splash under the muddy water. A split second later, Beaumont raised his gloved hand with the ball still in it. Then, the outfielder poked his head above the surface and, with a big grin, spit the dirty river water out of his mouth. ◇

★★★

George Altman of the Chicago Cubs walked—on three balls. In an April 24, 1960 game, the plate umpire called a balk on a 3-and-1 pitch and incorrectly awarded Altman first base.

Angels Take Batting Practice In Hotel Lobby!

...And Other Weird Batting Stories

Nightclub Singer Makes History...

The Only Girl to Bat In a Big League Game

The only woman ever to bat in a major league game was a nightclub singer named Kitty Burke. She actually hit a ball thrown by St. Louis Cardinals hurler Daffy Dean.

Kitty made baseball history on July 31, 1935, during a night game between the world champion Cardinals and the hometown Cincinnati Reds at Crosley Field. The game was played under unusual circumstances. Because it was oversold, about 10,000 fans were herded out onto the field to watch the game from foul territory. They jammed the foul lines from behind home plate to the outfield fences.

Kitty, a blonde blues singer and Cincinnati rooter, was among the fans on the field. She was standing only ten feet away from home plate when the Cardinals' Joe "Ducky" Medwick stepped up to the plate in the eighth inning. Kitty disliked the cocky Medwick, especially since he had scored on his last turn at bat to give the Cards the lead.

"You can't hit a lick!" she shouted at him. "You couldn't even hit the ball with an ironing board!"

Medwick scoffed back, "You couldn't hit if you were swinging an elephant!"

In the bottom of the eighth, Kitty was still fuming mad over Medwick's retort. So when the Reds' Babe Herman headed towards the batter's box, Kitty decided to take action.

"Hey, Babe!" she hollered. "Lend me your bat!"

"Go ahead," he replied.

Kitty, wearing a dress and high heels, marched up to the plate while the crowd roared with laughter. After

KITTY BURKE shows off her form.

taking a few practice swings, Kitty shouted to Dean, "Hey, you hick! Throw me a pitch!"

Dean stood on the mound, unsure what to do. By now, the crowd was in hysterics and shouting at Dean to throw the ball. Finally, the plate umpire yelled, "Play ball!"

So Dean lobbed the ball and Kitty smacked it—but right back to the mound. Dean fielded her tap and then, ungallantly, tagged out the only woman ever to bat in a major league game.

Kitty then ran back into the cheering crowd and into the history books. ◇

Ruth Caps Homer With Car Ride To the Dugout!

Babe Ruth clouted 714 home runs, but none was more stylish than the one he blasted in Boston in 1919. After finishing his home run trot, he rode in a car back to the dugout!

Babe, who was playing for the Boston Red Sox and making the transition from pitcher to outfielder, was given a special day by his legion of Beantown fans. As part of the pregame festivities, Ruth was presented with a new car.

Ruth, who always had a flair for the dramatic, waited until the last moment to charge up the crowd with some patented batting heroics on his special day.

In the bottom of the eighth inning, with Boston trailing 2-1, Ruth came to bat with a man on base—and belted a homer that ultimately won the game for the Red Sox, 3-2.

While the fans cheered their heads off, Ruth went into his distinctive, short-stepped home run trot. Not until he rounded third did he notice that his new car was motoring from the left field bleacher area to home plate.

After Ruth crossed the plate, the door to the car swung open and a chauffeur invited the slugger to step inside. Ruth was only too happy to oblige. Then, to the howls of laughter from the crowd, Ruth was given a chauffeur-driven ride—all the way back to the dugout. ◇

The Pop-Up That Never Came Down

Baffled Minnesota fielders John Castino (left) and Houston Jiminez wait in vain for a pop-up that never came down during a 1984 Twins home game. The ball, hit by Oakland's Dave Kingman, sailed through a hole in the fabric ceiling of the Metrodome for a ground-rule double.

Angels Take Batting Practice —In Lobby of Their Hotel!

The California Angels tried to squeeze in some extra batting practice in a most unusual place—the lobby of the Sheraton Boston Hotel.

Home plate was an ash tray. The right field fence was a bar and the left field barrier was a water fountain. The bats were made of plastic and the balls of foam rubber.

California tried the strange venue for BP in 1975 because of snide remarks made about the Angels' weak hitting. Texas Rangers manager Billy Martin had said the Angels could take batting practice in a hotel lobby for 30 minutes without breaking anything.

When the Angels arrived in Boston for a weekend series with the Red Sox, Boston hurler Bill Lee agreed with Martin, saying, "The Angels could hit in the lobby of the Grand Hotel and not break a chandelier."

So several California players tried some batting practice in their hotel lobby to prove the critics wrong. Well, the critics were right. The Angels didn't break anything, mostly because BP was cut short. With manager Dick Williams pitching and infielder Winston Llenas batting, a hotel security man ordered an end to the hijinks.

California could have used the extra batting practice. A few hours after the hotel lobby BP, Bill Lee shut out the Angels on five hits. ◇

An 'Ass-i-nine' Lineup

The Kansas City A's starting lineup is brought to the playing field on mules before a home game with the Minnesota Twins in 1965.

Baseball's First Midget Bats a Perfect 1.000

The first midget to play professional baseball banged out a hit in his only plate appearance before retiring with a perfect batting average of 1.000.

While most every fan assumes that Eddie Gaedel of the St. Louis Browns was the first little person to play professionally in 1951, the truth is that an actor named Jerry Sullivan appeared in a game nearly 50 years earlier.

In the final week of the 1905 season, George Stallings, manager of the fifth-place Buffalo Bisons of the Eastern League, struck up a friendship with Sullivan at the team's hotel in Baltimore. The midget, who was appearing in a musical called "Simple, Simon, Simple," was invited by Stallings to come to the ball park the next day and act as the club's mascot.

On September 18, Sullivan arrived in a Buffalo uniform and took to the coaching box for a couple of innings in the Bisons' game against the Orioles. In the ninth inning, with Buffalo trailing 10-2, Bisons catcher Frank McManus led off with a single. The pitcher was due up next. In an act of pure whimsy, Stallings sent his little pal to the plate as a pinch hitter.

Baltimore manager Hughie Jennings didn't object so Sullivan dug in at the batter's box as the crowd roared with laughter. So did the players. Baltimore pitcher Fred Burchell doubled over in a laughing fit. Finally, everyone settled down and Burchell fired his first pitch to Sullivan. It was high, naturally, for ball one.

He then threw the next pitch right down the middle, about six inches off the ground. To everyone's amazement, Sullivan hit the ball and blooped it over the third baseman's head for a single.

Burchell didn't find the midget funny anymore. He tried to pick him off first, but the little guy scurried back, ducking his head between the first

Midget Jerry Sullivan blooped the ball over third base for a single

baseman's legs. The next batter singled, sending Sullivan to second. Burchell was now so upset that he fired the next pitch five feet over the batter's head, and Sullivan rambled to third. He then scored on a single, punctuating the run with a headfirst slide into home which drew a tremendous ovation from the crowd. The Bisons rallied for four runs in the ninth, but still lost the game.

It was the only time Sullivan ever played. He returned to the stage, leaving behind an unblemished record in baseball—a perfect 1.000 batting average. ◇

Amazingly, there was once a pitcher who won more games in the World Series than he won in the regular season. Virgil (Fire) Trucks didn't win any games in the regular season for the Tigers in 1945—but he won a game in the World Series that year.

Batter Talks Official Scorer Out of Crediting Him With Hit

Future Hall-of-Famer Paul Waner needed only one more hit to reach baseball's milestone of 3,000. But when he got it, he demanded that it be ruled an error instead.

In 1942, with his spectacular career winding down, hits were not coming so easily to Big Poison anymore. He had gone hitless in 25 of the 52 games he had played that year for the Boston Braves.

In a game against the visiting Cincinnati Reds on June 17, Waner needed just one more hit to reach the cherished plateau. With teammate Tommy Holmes on first and running on the pitch, Waner chopped a ground ball towards short.

Cincinnati shortstop Eddie Joost, who had moved to his left to cover second, put on the brakes and headed back to his right, hoping to field the ball. Joost got a glove on the ball but couldn't hold it and both runners were safe. The Boston crowd waited to see how the play would be scored. All eyes were locked on the scoreboard, and when it read "hit," a huge roar went up. Umpire Beans Reardon called time and retrieved the ball. Then he hustled over to first base with the prized memento for Waner—but the player refused to accept it.

Instead, Waner cupped his hands around his mouth, looked up at the official scorer in the press box, and shouted, "Don't give me a hit. I don't want a hit on that play. I won't take it." Waner made such a fuss that the official scorer finally changed his ruling and gave Joost an error on the play. (It was no big deal to Joost. He finished the season with 50 errors).

"I'm glad about the ruling," Waner said after the game. "I want my 3,000th hit to be a clean one."

Two games later, he entered the 3,000 club when he rapped a solid single to center field off Rip Sewell of the Pittsburgh Pirates—his former team for 15 years.

Waner played two more seasons, collected a career total of 3,152 hits, and was inducted into the Baseball Hall of Fame in 1952. ◇

PAUL WANER refused to accept his tainted 3,000th hit.

Ted Williams Breaks Out of Slump by Swallowing Chaw

The great Ted Williams broke out of his worst batting slump ever in a sickening way—he got ill from chewing tobacco.

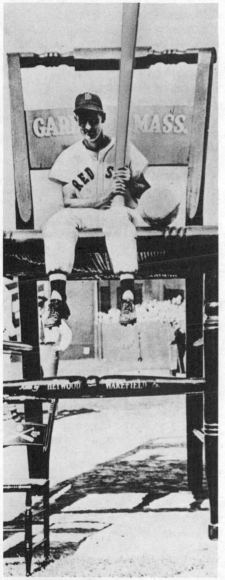

TED WILLIAMS carries a big stick.

As weird as that sounds, the Splendid Splinter credits a chaw of tobacco with helping get the hit he needed to bust out of his hitless skein.

During the 1954 season—after 12 consecutive years of hitting over .300—the Boston Red Sox star couldn't buy a hit. He fell into an 0-for-17 tailspin and wound up temporarily benched by manager Lou Boudreau.

The next day, the frustrated Williams was sitting on the bench during a game against the Washington Senators when he noticed the contentment on the face of teammate Grady Hatton. The infielder was happily chewing a cud of tobacco.

"I asked him to let me try some of that," Williams recalled. "So I took a chew, and spit and spit. Eventually I became very sick. I went to the clubhouse and took a drink of ginger ale. That made me even more nauseated."

Williams wanted to go into the clubhouse and lay down. He didn't care about the game or that Boston was trailing by two runs in the seventh inning. But just then, the Red Sox mounted a rally and had two men on base.

Boudreau immediately summoned Williams, slump and all, to go in and pinch-hit. "I was so sick I could hardly stand up when I went to the plate," Williams recalled. "But I got a line drive single. And that was the end of my slump."

Fortunately, Williams, whose career batting average was .344, had very few slumps—and he didn't have to get sick again to bust out of one. ◇

Batter Ejected After Hitting Game-Winning Home Run!

New York Yankees outfielder Roy "Stormy" Weatherly was given the old heave ho *after* the game was over—all because he belted a home run.

In 1943, the Yankees and the visiting Cleveland Indians were tied 3-3 when Weatherly came to the plate in the bottom of the ninth inning. He exchanged a few unpleasantries with plate umpire Cal Hubbard, with whom the player had been feuding the whole game.

Weatherly promptly knocked the

ROY WEATHERLY: Heave-ho homer.

first pitch of the inning into the right field stands to win the game.

But before he took off on his home run trot, Weatherly turned to Hubbard and said, "Well, you big bastard, how do you like that?"

Hubbard promptly replied, "You're out of the game!"

"Maybe so," said Weatherly, who then added smugly, "but not before I run around the bases."

Weatherly was not only tossed out of a game after it was over, he was also given the boot before a game even started.

When he was in the minors playing in the Evangeline League, he fell into a batting slump and didn't stroke a hit for two weeks.

Leading off a game in Warren, Texas, Weatherly belted the first pitch to right field for a double, but the plate umpire called him back.

"What's the matter?" the player asked.

"I didn't say, 'Play ball!' " replied the arbiter. "The hit doesn't count. We have to start over."

Weatherly flew into such a rage that the umpire ejected him from the game —one that officially hadn't even started yet. ◇

Gus Bell and his son Buddy are incredible examples of "like father, like son." Gus, who played in the majors from 1950-64, hit 206 homers and sported a lifetime batting average of .281. Buddy, who played from 1972-89, belted 201 homers and owned a career batting average of .279.

Yankee manager pinch-hits for two men in same inning

A major league manager inserted himself in the lineup as a pinch hitter —for two different players in the same inning!

New York Yankees skipper Frank Chance did it in a game against the St. Louis Browns on May 19, 1913. The Yankees were trailing 3-1 in the top of the eighth when Chance put himself in as a pinch hitter for his pitcher, Ray Fisher. Chance was hoping to get a rally started, but he promptly grounded out. However, the hitters who followed him started banging the ball all over the field.

The Yankees scored five runs and had runners on second and third when Chance grabbed a bat and went up to the plate for a second time in the same inning. This time he singled to left, driving in both runners.

After the next batter, Bert Daniels, grounded out, Lou Criger, the Browns' acting manager, came storming out to the plate. "Chance batted for two different men in this inning," Criger shouted to plate umpire George Hildebrand. "You've got to call somebody out."

The umpire then went back over the lineup. Sure enough, in his second at-bat in the frame, Chance had inadvertently pinch-hit for shortstop Claud Derrick, the Yankees' eighth-

FRANK CHANCE: Two chances.

place batter. Chance should have waited one more turn because he was hitting in the ninth-place spot.

Although Criger was right, his protest was too late. He should have complained before Daniels batted. So the runs counted and Chance's mistake helped seal a 10-3 win. ◇

Team Begins, Ends Game With Same Batting Averages

In the first and only time in major league history, all the players on a team finished a game sporting the exact same batting averages they began with.

It happened on Opening Day, 1939, when the Chicago White Sox fell victim to a no-hitter spun by the Cleveland Indians' young pitching sensation Bob Feller.

Chicago entered the game at Comiskey Park with a .000 batting average and each player on the roster had a .000 average. At the end of the game, everything was still the same—the team still had the same .000 batting average.

Major League's Best Hitter Lasts Just One Game!

The player with the best batting average in major league history never got a chance to prove how good he really was.

He lasted only one day in the bigs.

More than 20 players have hit a perfect 1.000 in their major league careers, but only one—John Paciorek—owns a perfect batting average after hitting more than twice.

Paciorek was a strapping, 6-foot, 2-inch, 200-pound 18-year-old outfielder from Detroit when he joined the Houston Astros at the end of the 1963 season.

In the year's final game, Paciorek made a stunning debut. He played flawlessly in the outfield and got on base every time he batted. He came to the plate five times, walked twice and stroked three singles. He also drove in three runs and scored four times as Houston beat the New York Mets 13-4.

The rookie—whose younger brother Tom later embarked on an 18-year career in the majors—impressed veterans, management, and longtime baseball observers.

"Paciorek should be a cinch to make it as a big leaguer," wrote reporter Gus Maucuso in *The Houston Post.* "He shows promise of becoming a great hitter. He swings the bat with authority and shows good speed in the outfield and on the bases, too."

But during spring training the following year, Paciorek didn't survive the final cut, and the Astros sent him back to the minors. He never returned to the bigs. His playing days were over after he suffered back problems that grew progressively worse until he was forced to undergo career-ending back surgery in 1967.

But his 3-for-3 lifetime batting performance still makes John Paciorek statistically the best hitter in the history of major league baseball. ◇

JOHN PACIOREK: Short career.

Batter Gets 2 Hits on Same Day—785 Miles Apart!

Joel Youngblood hit safely for two different teams on the same day.

On Aug. 4, 1982, Youngblood collected one hit for the New York Mets against the Cubs in a day game in Chicago before learning that he had just been traded to the Montreal Expos. Then he flew to Philadelphia to join the Expos, who played the Phillies later that night. In that game, he singled in his only at-bat.

That gave Youngblood two hits for two different teams against two different foes in two different cities—all on the same day.

Catcher Picks Off Runner — With a Potato!

...And Other Stories of Incredible Plays

Runner Gunned Down at Home By Peg From Opponent's Coach

St. Louis Browns coach Jimmy Austin became the tenth—and sneaki-est—man on the team when he fielded an errant throw by the dugout and threw out a runner at the plate.

Incredibly, Austin got away with it!

In the fifth inning of a 1927 game, the visiting Washington Senators had runner Sam Rice on first base and Goose Goslin at the plate. Goslin smacked a line drive past the shortstop and onto the outfield grass which was still wet from a heavy morning rain.

Browns left fielder Bing Miller raced to his right, scooped up the ball and fired it toward third base, hoping to nail Rice. But because of the wet field, the ball was slippery and Miller's throw flew wildly over the head of third baseman Frank O'Rourke. The ball then caromed off the low wall in front of the box seats and rolled in front of Coach Austin, who was standing on the steps of the Browns' dugout.

Meanwhile, Rice had rounded third and was steaming for the plate as Browns pitcher Milt Gaston pursued the errant throw. Gaston was about 20 feet away from the ball when Austin did the unthinkable.

Maybe it was because he had played

Tape Silences Vocal Slugger

Normally vocal Dave Parker of the Pittsburgh Pirates wears a piece of trainer's tape over his mouth during batting practice before a 1979 game. Parker, who enjoyed needling teammates and opponents alike, jokingly was told to keep his mouth shut by a fellow Pirate. So Parker slapped on the tape. But his self-imposed silence lasted only ten minutes before he was teasing teammates again.

third base for 14 years in the bigs, and just couldn't resist fielding a ball. But whatever the reason, Austin reached down, grabbed the ball, and fired a strike to catcher Wally Schang, who tagged the sliding Rice.

"Yer out!" the umpire yelled.

The Senators erupted in protest, arguing that the Browns' coach had thrown the ball to the plate, not the pitcher, as the ump erroneously thought. But the Washington pleas fell on deaf ears. The umpire had made the call and he wasn't about to change it. Through the brouhaha, Austin sat quietly in the dugout, looking as innocent as a harp-twanging angel.

Miller recalled that the next day he looked at the box score in the morning newspaper, thinking maybe Austin had been given an assist on the play. "He deserved one," said Miller. ◇

Home Run Ball Travels More Than 100 Miles!

St. Louis Cardinals pitcher Wish Egan served up the longest home run in major league history—the ball traveled over 100 miles!

On July 15, 1905, the visiting Cardinals were playing the Boston Braves (then known as the Nationals) at the old South End Grounds. Egan, who was hardly an ace (he finished the season with a woeful 6-15 mark), felt his curve ball looked good during his warmup. So he decided to throw it against the first batter he faced, Boston outfielder Jim Delahanty.

But Egan hung his curve ball and Delahanty smacked it with all his might. The ball soared so high and deep over the left field wall that outfielder Spike Shannon didn't even budge. The ball sailed out of the park, took one big bounce by the New York, New Haven & Hartford Railroad tracks, and plopped right into a gondola car of a moving freight train that was chugging south. Someone finally retrieved the ball when the train reached the end of the line in Willimantic, Connecticut—over 100 miles away from home plate!

Incredibly, Egan served up the majors' second-longest homer to the very next batter. Still showing faith in his curve ball, Egan fired a bender to Boston third baseman Harry Wolverton. Once again, the hurler hung his curve and Wolverton blasted another tape-measure homer, this time over the right field wall and onto Columbus Avenue.

"The ball landed in a fat lady's lap in an open car bound for City Point, South Boston," recalled Egan. "Two pitches, two home runs—one good for over 100 miles and the other for six.

"And now I hold the dubious distinction of giving up the two longest home-run balls on record." ◇

★★★

Padres Get Three Kevins for One

In 1986, the San Diego Padres traded Kevin McReynolds to the New York Mets for Kevin Mitchell, Kevin Armstrong, and Kevin Brown!

Makes Best Catch of All...

Player marries fan after falling in her lap when chasing foul ball

A foul ball found a fair lady for first baseman Norm Zauchin.

He fell over a low railing while pursuing a foul ball and ended up in the lap of a pretty fan. Zauchin made the catch—in more ways than one. He not only caught the ball, but captured the heart of the young woman—and wound up marrying her!

Before Zauchin became a young star with the Boston Red Sox in the 1950s, he played first base for the Birmingham Barons, Boston's farm team. At 6-feet, 4-inches and 220 pounds, Zauchin was a hot power-hitting prospect aiming to make it to "the show"—the big leagues.

One hot Sunday afternoon in 1950 at sold-out Rickwood Stadium in Birmingham, Zauchin was playing first with his usual total concentration. He failed to notice a pretty brown-haired, blue-eyed high school senior sitting with her parents in the front row of box seats next to the first base dugout. Her name was Janet Mooney.

She wasn't much of a baseball fan but because she just had a fight with her boyfriend and was feeling down, Janet decided half-heartedly to go to the Sunday baseball game with her parents.

Suddenly, in the middle of the game, a fan yelled, "Look out! The ball is coming our way!" A lazy pop foul was heading right toward Janet.

With his eyes locked on the ball, Zauchin raced to the railing and reached into the stands as far as he could. He snared the ball with a great backhanded stab—and then flipped over the railing and tumbled right in the lap of the startled and frightened young woman.

While the crowd roared with laughter, Zauchin lay on Janet's lap and looked up at her big blue eyes, grinned, and said, "Hi!" Janet was too stunned to answer. Afraid he'd squish her if he stayed any longer, the hulking player rolled off her lap, climbed over the railing, and returned to his position.

But for the rest of the game, Zauchin just couldn't keep his mind on baseball. He kept glancing over at Janet, admiring her soft, pretty face and gentle eyes. She in turn immediately discovered a whole new interest in baseball—and in the tall, handsome first baseman.

It was love at first sight.

In those days, it was customary for families in Birmingham to invite ballplayers home for Sunday dinner. After the game, Zauchin learned that the box seat usher knew the parents of the girl on whom he had fallen head over heels. So the usher wrangled an

★★★

In 1956, Boston Red Sox batter Frank Sullivan hit into a double play and drove in a run—without being charged with a time at bat. He hit a sacrifice fly to right, scoring a runner from third. But a runner on first was out trying to tag up and go to second.

66

invitation for Zauchin and him to have dinner with the Mooneys. From that day on, neither Zauchin nor Janet dated anyone else.

Although they both wanted to get married, they agreed to wait until Zauchin made it to the majors when he'd have enough money to support Janet and start a family. Secure in knowing he had found the right girl, Zauchin played with incredible determination to fulfill two dreams—reach the majors and marry Janet.

The following year, while playing for the AAA Louisville Colonels, the day every minor leaguer yearns for arrived for Zauchin. He was called into the manager's office after a game and told,

"Pack your bags. You're going to 'the show.'"

The words were hardly out of the manager's mouth when Zauchin bolted to the nearest phone and called Janet. "Honey," he shouted. "Set the date!"

"Lord have mercy!" Janet screamed. "You're going to the majors! Now we can finally get married!"

They wed six months later. Today Norm and Janet Zauchin are happily married grandparents living in Bessemer, Alabama.

Asked if he ever wondered what would have happened had he not pursued that foul ball, Zauchin said, "Maybe I'd still be a bachelor." ◊

Phillies Pitcher Makes a Big Splash With Fans

Philadelphia Phillies prankster and pitcher Roger McDowell cools off some Wrigley Field Bleacher Bums with a big bucket of water before a Chicago Cubs home game on a hot summer afternoon in 1990.

Yankees Score Run *After* Third Out!

In one of the rarest plays witnessed in major league history, the New York Yankees scored a run *after* making the third out.

And the only way to have prevented the run was if the Milwaukee Brewers had retired the Yankees on a fourth out!

As impossible as it seems, New York scored a legitimate run after the inning was over during a 1989 game—one in which the players and fans didn't even realize the run had counted until the game was over.

Here's how the strange play unfolded:

With one out in the eighth inning, the Yankees were at bat leading the Brewers 4-1. Mike Pagliarulo was on third and Bob Geren on first when Yankees manager Dallas Green ordered batter Wayne Tolleson to attempt a suicide squeeze.

Pagliarulo broke for home with the pitch—and Tolleson popped it up.

"Pags" was literally on top of the plate when pitcher Jay Aldrich caught the ball in the air and then threw it to first to double off Geren. That made three outs and ended the inning, right? Wrong.

Unknown to everybody except home plate umpire Larry Barnett, Pagliarulo had scored on the play. Doubling a runner off base is not a continuous action double play, so the run could count.

Pagliarulo had obviously left third base before the ball was caught and hadn't tagged up, so he should have been called out for that reason, right? Wrong.

The only way he could have been called out was on an appeal.

That's where the fourth out comes in. Milwaukee had to throw the ball to third base and appeal Pagliarulo's run

Umpire Ejects Reporters From Press Box

When National League umpire Bruce Froemming was a 19-year-old freshman arbiter working in the Northern League in the 1950s, he cleared an entire press box.

During a game in Duluth, Minnesota, Froemming had been the object of verbal abuse from reporters who were yelling at him from the press box. After the game, Froemming warned them to keep their mouths shut the next time...or else.

The following night he overruled a call by a fellow ump at second base. The writers went nuts, shouting epithets at Froemming. When they ignored his orders to stop, he gave them the old heave-ho.

But the reporters refused to leave the press box. So the young, headstrong ump yanked the two teams off the field—and told the scribes he would forfeit the game to the visiting St. Cloud club if they weren't out of the press box in ten minutes. They left.

before every infielder, including the pitcher, crossed the foul lines into foul territory.

Since they didn't appeal the play, the run counted.

"It's rule 7.10d," explained Barnett after the game. "It's the apparent fourth-out rule where the defense has to appeal the play.

"They didn't do that, and it's not my job to tell them. So the run counted."

The players, managers, fans, and even the official scorer didn't know the rule. Since the real final score—Yankees 5, Brewers 1—wasn't posted until long after the game, the fans went home thinking the Yankees had won 4-1.

Said manager Green, "I've been in this game for 33 years, and I've never, ever, ever seen a play like that." ◇

Manager's Praying Doesn't Budge Umpire

American Association umpire Walter Peters gives the heave-ho sign to Louisville manager Jack Tighe, who appears to be pleading in prayer fashion to stay around. But the umpire gave him the boot for disputing a play at first base in a game against Oklahoma City in 1962.

Cubs runner thrown out at plate by mistake—on wild peg to first

The St. Louis Cardinals' Ed Konetchy threw a runner out at the plate by mistake—while trying to nail another runner at first base!

The freaky play occured in the first inning of a 1911 game between the visiting Cardinals and the Chicago Cubs.

With Cubs runner Jimmy Sheckard on second base and two outs, batter

Frank Chance drilled a hot shot at Konetchy who was playing first base. Konetchy, who was poised near the edge of the outfield grass, knocked the ball down and it trickled into foul territory.

As Cardinals pitcher Bob Harmon raced over to cover the bag, Sheckard dashed around third and streaked for home.

Konetchy thought he still had enough time to get Chance at first base for the final out by throwing the ball to Harmon. But in his haste, Konetchy fired a bullet that sailed past Harmon and flew toward home plate.

Meanwhile, Cardinals catcher Roger Bresnahan was standing at the plate watching the play at first base when he saw the ball making a beeline toward him. He caught the ball just in time to tag the onrushing Sheckard for the putout, ending a scoreless inning for the Cubs.

In an account of the game the next day, *The Chicago Tribune* said, "Making a throw to get one runner at first base and unexpectedly getting a different one at the plate is quite new in baseball. It shows the great possibilities of the national pastime." ◇

Second Baseman Nose How to Show Off!

Julio Cruz of the White Sox warms up with a balancing act during batting practice before a game with Kansas City in 1983.

70

Catcher Picks Off Runner—With a Potato!

In the most outrageous pickoff play in professional baseball, a catcher tricked a runner by throwing a potato. But it was the catcher who ultimately was put out—of a job.

With three games left in the 1987 season, the Williamsport Bills of the Class AA Eastern League were in seventh place 27 games out of first. So catcher Dave Bresnahan decided to liven up the dull end-of-the-year contest with a potato prank.

Before a game with the Reading Phillies, he carved a potato to look like a baseball and hid it in his mitt. During the contest, Reading runner Rick Lundblade took a lead off third base. That's when Bresnahan whipped out the potato and deliberately fired it over the third baseman's head. Lundblade, thinking the spud was a ball, bolted for home, only to be tagged out by Bresnahan who had the real ball in his glove. "You should have seen the look on the guy's face when he came home," the catcher recalled.

The fans laughed, but the umpire didn't. He ruled Lundblade safe at home and then ejected the fun-loving catcher. Although the Bills won the game 4-3, Bills manager Orlando Gomez had zero tolerance for a 25-year-old second-string backstop with a .149 batting average. Quicker than you can say french fry, Bresnahan was benched and fined $50. Two days later the Cleveland Indians, the Bills' parent club, chastised him as "unprofessional" and released him.

"Well, now I can run for governor of

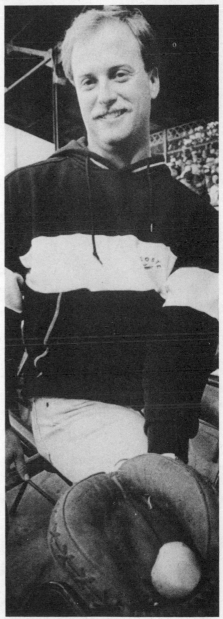

DAVE BRESNAHAN'S 'hot' potato.

Idaho," quipped the great nephew of Hall of Fame catcher Roger Bresnahan. "I was surprised at their reaction. I mean, it's not like it was the seventh game of the World Series. Besides, there's nothing in the rule book that says you can't throw a potato."

A year later, all was forgiven. The Bills decided to honor Bresnahan with baseball immortality.

They retired the catcher's number, gave him a night, and allowed fans to get in for $1 and a potato, many of which he autographed.

His No. 59 is the only one hanging on the outfield fence at Bowman Field in Williamsport today.

The night his number was retired, the infamous play was reenacted and Bresnahan, who is now nicknamed Spuds, was given the key to the city.

"I remember an old movie about Lou Gehrig when his number was retired," Bresnahan told fans. "He said he felt like the luckiest man on the face of the earth. I feel even luckier because Gehrig had to hit .340 and play in more than 2,000 consecutive games to get his number retired.

All I had to do was hit less than .150 and throw a potato." ◇

"Willie the Robot" Learns from the Pros

"Weekend Willie," a mechanical robot at the Naval Air Reserve Training Station in Jacksonville, Florida, gets some pitching instructions from Joe Dodson (left) and Jack Kramer of the Boston Red Sox. "Willie" visited the major leaguers when they played an exhibition game in 1949.

Cubs Batter 'Plasters' Homer

...In Wet Cement!

Chicago Cubs slugger Cy Williams clouted a long fair ball that landed in a pile of wet cement. By the time the now-heavy, cement-encased ball was retrieved, Williams had an inside-the-park home run.

The hard ball game was played in 1916 at the Baker Bowl, home of the Philadelphia Phillies. Groundskeeper Sam Payne had a small locker against the fence in right center field where he kept his tools. Before the game against the Cubs, Payne filled some cracks with cement at the base of the wall. He then put a bucket of the wet cement inside the tool locker, but forgot to close the door all the way.

The open door went unnoticed until the fifth inning when Williams smacked a long liner past Phillies center fielder Dode Paskert.

Incredibly, the ball bounced twice and disappeared inside the tool locker.

In a frantic search, Paskert reached into the locker and started tossing aside buckets, shovels, and tools. But he couldn't find the ball. Finally he plunged his hand into the bucket of wet cement, fished around for a moment, and came up with the ball.

Although it was thoroughly plastered, Paskert threw the ball, cement and all, back toward the infield. But the ball was so heavy it didn't even reach the cutoff man. It didn't matter anyway. Williams had already touched home. ◇

Pitcher walks batter he never even faced!

Pittsburgh Pirates hurler Dock Ellis walked a batter he never faced!

The bizarre play happened in 1973 when Ellis was struggling in a game against the Atlanta Braves. After Dock threw two pitches way out of the strike zone to Braves batter Sonny Jackson, Pirates manager Bill Virdon decided he'd seen enough of Ellis for the day. Virdon replaced Dock, a right-hander, with the lefty Ramon Hernandez.

Braves manager Eddie Mathews then countered by sending up right-handed batter Dick Dietz to pinch-hit for Jackson. Hernandez proceeded to walk Dietz—or at least that's the way it seemed.

But that's not the way it's scored.

According to the scoring rules of baseball, the hurler who delivers the first two balls to a batter and then is replaced is charged with a walk if the relief pitcher throws balls three and four.

But in Dock's case, the batter who drew the walk wasn't the one he was pitching to. Nevertheless, the scoring rules state that the batter who gets the last two balls is given credit for a walk.

So Ellis was charged with walking Dietz—even though the hurler never faced him. ◇

★★★

Jackie Price, a Cleveland Indians coach in the late 1940s, could throw two balls at the same time with one hand—one a fastball, the other a curve.

73

Warmup pitch belted for homer

John "Stuffy" McInnis hit the sneakiest home run of all time. He clubbed an inside-the-park round-tripper—off a warmup pitch!

And it was legal.

In 1911, American League president Ban Johnson decided the games were getting too long. He feared that if there was too much down time between innings, fans would get bored and attendance would drop. So he decreed

...and it counted!

that pitchers could no longer throw warmup pitches between innings once the batter reached the plate.

Because the rule was so unpopular, it was seldom enforced and most players soon forgot about it.

But one player who didn't forget was Philadelphia Athletics first baseman Stuffy McInnis.

McInnis was slated to lead off the top of the eighth with the A's leading 6-3 over the Boston Red Sox at Fenway Park on June 27, 1911. It was a hot day and the players were still listlessly changing sides when Boston hurler Ed Karger—the first to take his position—lobbed a warmup toss to catcher Les Nunamaker, who had just moved behind the plate.

McInnis stood a few feet away, acting as though he wasn't paying any attention. But then he casually inched toward the plate as Karger tossed a second warmup lob.

Suddenly, McInnis jumped into the batter's box and belted the ball to center field.

It wasn't a particularly hard hit—but there was no one in center field. Or in left or right for that matter. The Boston fielders were still strolling out to their positions. In fact, two Philadelphia players, left fielder Bris Lord and second baseman Eddie Collins, had yet to reach the A's dugout when McInnis hit the warmup pitch.

The Red Sox stood frozen as they watched the ball roll towards the fence. Meanwhile, McInnis dashed merrily

JOHN McINNIS merrily circled the bases after hitting a homer.

around the bases and touched home plate long before anyone even bothered to retrieve the ball.

The Boston players charged the umpire, demanding he declare the hit illegal and make McInnis bat again. But the man in blue ruled the hit was a valid home run. He reminded the Red Sox that President Johnson's new edict said a pitcher could not throw a warmup pitch once an opposing player reached the batter's box. Thus, he said, McInnis had a right to hit the ball.

The controversial home run had no effect on the game, which the A's won 7-3. But it did convince Johnson to abandon his game-shortening edict—because he didn't want to ever see another homer hit off a warmup pitch. ◇

The Majors' Weirdest Play!

Runner Tagged at Plate With Ball Stuck in a Tomato Can!

In one of the most bizarre plays in baseball history, a runner was tagged with a ball stuck in a tomato can!

It happened in a National League game between the Boston Braves and Cleveland Spiders in 1892 at the Congress Street Park in Boston. The ball park was unusual because it had no outfield fence. Instead, the outfield was bordered by a garbage dump filled with trash and old tin cans.

The score was tied 2-2 in the top of the ninth inning when Cleveland's Jimmy McAleer belted a line drive so hard that it flew past Braves centerfielder Hugh Duffy and slammed into a pile of cans in the dump.

Duffy raced over to the spot where the ball had landed. But to his shock, he discovered that the ball had wound up smack inside a rusty tomato can. Try as he might, he couldn't yank that ball out. It was stuck!

By now, McAleer was rounding second base. Duffy had to do something fast. In desperation, he picked up the can—with the ball still stuck inside—and heaved it to teammate Billy Nash at third base. But it was too late. McAleer had already rounded the bag and was steaming for home with the winning run.

When Nash caught the tomato can, he looked at it in amazement for a split second, then relayed it with rifle-like velocity to catcher Charlie Bennett at the plate.

Bennett snared the can and put the tag on McAleer as the Cleveland runner slid across the plate. Boston fans yelled and whooped because Bennett had clearly tagged McAleer before he reached home. But even though the umpire saw the ball in the tomato can, he insisted that McAleer was safe.

When the Braves began to argue, the ump lifted his hand to silence them and said, "Gentlemen, since when is a runner out just because he's been tagged with a rusty tomato can?" ◇

During the 1930s, New York Giants head groundskeeper Marty Schwab lived and worked at the Polo Grounds. The Giants built an apartment for Schwab and his family under Section 31 in left field.

Batter Is Put Out by a Snowball!

Cleveland infielder Ray Boone was robbed of an extra base hit when he was put out—by a snowball!

It happened in a 1953 exhibition game in Denver when the Indians, managed by Al Lopez, were playing the New York Giants. A heavy snow storm had hit the day before the game. Snow plows had cleared the field, but they left a giant snow bank all around the outfield about 15 feet in front of the fence.

"We agreed that any ball hit between the snow bank and the fence would be a ground rule double," Lopez recalled.

The game was played without incident until Boone stepped to the plate and hit a deep fly to right. Giants right fielder George Wilson went back for the ball and then tumbled over the

snow bank and fell out of sight.

Just as Boone was rounding first, Wilson arose with his glove held high over his head with a very white ball nestled in the middle of his mitt. The first base umpire signalled that Boone was out. But the "white" wasn't the baseball—it was a snowball! Wilson had packed the snow, put it in his glove, and fooled the umpire.

"Wilson never caught the ball," insisted Lopez. "He didn't even come close. I yelled and yelled about it, but the umpire still called Boone out."

Wilson, meanwhile, surreptitiously retrieved the real ball a few seconds later and trotted in. And Boone had the dubious honor of being the only major leaguer ever called out because of a snowball. ◇

World's Largest Catcher's Mitt!

Al Schacht, "The Clown Prince of Baseball," wears the world's largest catcher's mitt—2½ feet by 1½ feet. Schacht, who also uses the frame of a fan for a mask, donated the glove to the Baseball Hall of Fame.

The Uniform Number From Hell!

...And Other Unusual Stories of Uniforms And Equipment

Braves Win World Series 'Scuff-le' With Shoe Shine

The Milwaukee Braves won the pivotal game of the 1957 World Series—thanks largely to a reserve infielder's newly-shined shoes.

The Braves, down two games to one to the powerful New York Yankees, were one pitch away from a 4-1 victory when Elston Howard blasted a stunning three-run homer with two out in the top of the ninth inning.

After the shellshocked Braves failed to score in the bottom of the frame, New York's Hank Bauer tripled Tony Kubek home for the go-ahead run in the top of the tenth.

Things looked grim for the Braves. It was up to pinch-hitter Nippy Jones to ignite his now-devastated team. The seldom-used 32-year-old reserve first baseman had been called up from the minors late in the season.

Now here he was in a World Series game, facing Yankees reliever Tommy Byrne, a hurler known for wildness. Byrne's first pitch was low and inside and got by Berra as Jones tried to dance out of the way.

The batter started toward first base but was called back by umpire Augie Donatelli. "I was hit in the foot by the pitch," Jones insisted. Donatelli didn't see it that way and a fierce argument raged for several minutes.

Suddenly, Jones bent down and picked up the ball, which had rebounded off the backstop. "Here!" he shouted at the ump. "Look at the shoe polish on the ball!"

Big as life, there was a black splotch on the ball. The umpire looked down at Jones' polished black shoes, eyed the ball again, and waved Jones to first base.

The shoeshine pitch ignited the Braves. Shortstop Johnny Logan followed with a double, scoring the pinch runner put in for Jones. Then,

NIPPY JONES (25) shows Umpire Donatelli the ball that hit his shoe.

with the score tied, Eddie Mathews swatted a dramatic home run, vaulting Milwaukee to an amazing 7-5 victory and tying the Series at two games each. The pumped-up Braves went on to "polish" off the Yankees in seven games and win the Series.

But if it hadn't been for Nippy Jones and his freshly-shined baseball shoes, Milwaukee might never have won. Twelve years later, New York Mets batter Cleon Jones was involved in a similar "scuffle" in the fifth and final game of the 1969 World Series.

Umpire Lou DiMuro called a ball on a pitch that Jones claimed had hit him. After Jones showed the ump shoe polish on the ball, he was awarded first base. A moment later, Jones scored on a homer by Donn Clendenon in the Mets' 5-3 victory. ◇

Bad Hop Turns Single Into...

INSIDE-THE-POCKET HOMER!

St. Louis Browns outfielder Cliff Carroll was a victim of an inside-the-pocket home run that led to a change in uniforms.

Before the turn of the century, players' uniforms sported breast pockets on shirts. But that soon changed because of the misfortune that befell Carroll.

During a game in St. Louis in 1892, Chicago Cubs infielder Bad Bill Dahlen rapped a single down the right field line. Carroll raced in, hoping to cut the ball off and hold Dahlen to a single. But the ball took a bad hop, bounced up, and hit Carroll in the chest. As he grabbed wildly for the ball, Carroll inadvertently shoved it down into the pocket of his uniform shirt.

The ball was so deep in his pocket that he couldn't get it out. Carroll tugged frantically at the ball, but it just wouldn't budge.

Meanwhile, Dahlen, a speedster and one of the league's leading base stealers, saw Carroll's predicament and dashed around first base. Carroll panicked and started running to second while still desperately trying to get the ball out of his pocket. Dahlen sprinted past second and kept right on going with Carroll in hot pursuit. When Dahlen rounded third and headed for home, Carroll stopped and, with one last Herculean effort, finally managed to free the ball from his little shirt pocket. But his throw home was much too late. Dahlen had "pocketed" a home run.

St. Louis owner Chris von der Ahe was in such a fury over the incident that he ordered all the pockets removed from every Browns' uniform shirt. Other owners soon followed the club's example to make sure that what happened to Cliff Carroll would never happen to one of their players. ◇

We Wuz Robbed!

The Kansas City Royals wear a mixture of uniforms in a 1977 game after a thief broke into a clubhouse in Milwaukee and took their shirts and warmup jackets. Most Royals wore Brewers uniforms.

No. 15 a Jinx to Tigers...

The uniform number from

HELL

Pain and suffering—and near tragedy—plagued any Detroit Tigers player who, between 1948 and 1950, dared to wear No. 15.

Relief pitcher Johnny Gorsica was the first Tiger to fall victim to the uniform number from hell. After compiling a 2-0 record in 1947, the seven-year veteran donned No. 15. He immediately suffered arm problems in spring training and was promptly released. Gorsica never pitched in the majors again.

Fellow hurler Art Houtteman was the next Tiger to put on the jinxed number before the start of the 1948 season. Houtteman, coming off a fine 7-2 season in 1947, was looking forward to a great year. Instead, he lived a pitcher's nightmare—by losing his first eight games, many by scores of 1-0 and 2-1.

By June, Houtteman was desperate to switch uniform numbers with any teammate who was willing to do so. At first, he couldn't find a taker because, as fellow pitcher Dizzy Trout told him, "That number's no good."

However, George Kell, Tigers third baseman and team captain, scoffed at the thought the uniform was jinxed. "I'll switch numbers with you, Art," said Kell. "I don't believe in all that stuff about bad luck numbers." So Kell swapped his No. 21 for Houtteman's No. 15.

The hurler finally recorded his first victory of the season after the number switch. Kell, however, wasn't so fortunate. During a game against the New York Yankees, a line drive off the bat of Joe DiMaggio smashed into Kell's jaw and sidelined the Tiger for the final month of the season. The

ART HOUTTEMAN'S number was up.

skeptic turned into a believer in the black-cloud powers of No. 15 and refused to wear it again. "Too much tough luck goes with it," said Kell. "I don't want any part of it."

At spring training the following year, Houtteman gave Kell back his old uniform number and put in a request for a new number. To his shock, the pitcher was handed his old No. 15. He put up a tremendous howl until the club offered to give him a different number. But since new uniforms weren't going to be ready for two weeks, he reluctantly agreed to wear No. 15 temporarily.

Nine days later, Houtteman lay close

to death in a Florida hospital with a fractured skull after a collision between his convertible and a trailer-truck. He survived the near-fatal accident and returned to the mound two months later—but with a different uniform number.

Tigers first baseman Paul Campbell, a five-year major league veteran, was the next player foolish enough to wear No. 15. Campbell didn't have it long. He was sold to a minor league club and never played in the bigs again.

To end the curse of No. 15, team trainer Jack Homel packed the uniform in an old trunk. By the time the number was worn again years later, its evil powers had vanished. ◊

Cubs Fielder Plays in Bathrobe!

Dan Friend played left field in the ninth inning of a National League game—wearing a bathrobe! The only sign of a uniform was the baseball cap perched on his head.

"The game should be forfeited!" New York Giants manager Scrappy Joyce screamed at umpire Bob Emslie. But despite the weird sight in the outfield, the arbiter insisted the game go on.

The bizarre incident occurred on Aug. 30, 1897, in New York. The Chicago Cubs were leading 7-5 at the end of eight innings when player-manager Cap Anson demanded Emslie call the game because of darkness. Emslie refused.

Anson was still steaming mad as he came up to bat in the top of the ninth. When Emslie called a strike on him, Anson exploded and was promptly tossed out of the game. The fiery manager then refused to send up a pinch hitter to finish his at-bat, so Emslie declared Anson the first out of the inning.

In the bottom of the ninth, as the day grew darker, the umpire ordered the Cubs to hurry to their positions. Left fielder George Decker took Anson's place at first base. But there was no one in left. All eyes were riveted on the Chicago dugout. The crowd waited to see who would play left because Anson—in his rage—had sent all his substitutes to the showers at the end of the eighth inning.

Finally a figure emerged, attired in a bathrobe of light gray material, buttoned all the way down the front. It was Dan Friend, a left-handed pitcher who had not suited up that day. When ordered into the game, he didn't have time to change from his street clothes, so he threw on the robe. The only thing close to a uniform was his cap.

Joyce stormed out of the Giants dugout and reminded Emslie of the rule which states no one but uniformed players could take part in a game. He demanded the Cubs forfeit. Emslie refused and shouted, "Play ball!"

When the first two New York batters were retired in the ninth, Joyce confronted the ump again, claiming that the robe-clad Friend was violating the rules.

"How do I know he doesn't have a uniform on under the robe?" Emslie reasoned. "What do you want me to do, search him?"

"You're darn right," said Joyce. "Go out and look."

At that point, Emslie pulled out his watch, looked at the time and then the sky—and declared the game called on account of darkness.

It was the first and last time a player dressed in a bathrobe appeared in a major league game. ◊

He Wears Flesh-Colored Mitts...
Fielder Uses Glove on Each Hand

The first professional player to use a glove actually wore two at the same time—one on each hand!

Not only that but he was so worried about being called a sissy that he dyed the gloves the color of flesh in the hopes that no one would notice.

In the early days of baseball, players didn't wear gloves, batting helmets, or any other protective gear. As far as they were concerned, only a pantywaist worried about hurting his hands.

But one player who did worry was Charles C. Waitt, outfielder for St. Louis of the National Association—baseball's first professional league. In 1875, he decided a glove would help him catch the ball and ease the pain of snaring line drives barehanded. However, Waitt didn't want the fans to notice he was wearing a glove for fear their taunting would drive him to distraction.

The last thing he wanted was to be called a sissy.

So he designed a very small leather glove that looked similar to today's typical golf glove. And he dyed it flesh color to make it inconspicuous. Then he figured that if one glove was good, a pair would be even better. He had a second one made for his throwing hand with the fingers cut off so it wouldn't impede his grip on the ball.

Waitt only played a few games wearing gloves on both hands. Despite their flesh color and small size, his gloves were noticed by other players—and fans—who jeered and ridiculed him.

Nevertheless, Waitt had set in motion a revolution in baseball. Within two years, gloves were becoming common on the playing field, thanks to Chicago Cubs star Al Spalding, one of the game's best players back then. He thought gloves were not only a good idea but a profitable one since he and his brother owned a sporting goods business in Chicago.

To boost sales of this new sporting equipment, Spalding wanted everyone to know that he was wearing a pair of gloves when he played—so he colored them black. When fans didn't taunt the renowned Spalding, it quickly became acceptable for players to wear gloves on both hands.

Eventually, as gloves became bigger, they were only used on the non-throwing hand. Today's webbed, dyed, leather mitts are monstrosities compared to the tiny flesh-colored gloves worn by a player who dared to be different. ◇

Team Owner's 'Number' Retired

Gene Autry is the only team owner ever to have his number retired. Autry, owner of the California Angels, had No. 26 retired in his honor after the Angels won the 1982 American League Western Division.

The team voted to so honor Autry, and picked No. 26 because they felt the former "Singing Cowboy" was so important to them that he was like the team's "26th man." Rosters are limited to 25 players.

Hitter Wields Table Leg for Bat!

After striking out twice against fire-balling hurler Nolan Ryan, Detroit Tigers first baseman Norm Cash tried a new bat during his next trip to the plate—a table leg!

In a 1973 game, Ryan, pitching for the California Angels, was gunning for his second no-hitter of the year when Cash decided to have some fun. He went into the clubhouse, grabbed the sawed-off leg of an old table, and sauntered to the plate with the leg on his shoulder in the ninth inning.

After a good laugh, the umpire sent Cash back for a real bat. It didn't do Norm much good. He struck out again and Ryan hurled another no-hitter.

Cash wasn't the first hitter to wield a wacky bat. In 1929, Rabbit Maranville, of the Boston Braves, once came to the plate with a tennis racquet to try to snap a personal batting slump against Dazzy Vance.

Like Cash, Rabbit had no success in convincing the umpire to let him use his zany club. And like Cash, Rabbit returned with legal lumber and promptly struck out. ◇

Number Seven Spells His Name Backwards

John Neves, a second baseman for Fargo-Moorhead of the Northern League, wore No. 7 backwards on his jersey in 1951 not only to be different but because, that way, it spelled out his name.

Astros Lineup Card Delivered In Frying Pan

Houston Astros captain Doug Rader once delivered his team's starting lineup to the plate umpire in a big iron frying pan!

And he did it while wearing a tall chef's hat and sporting an apron over his uniform.

Rader wanted to cook up something special for "Short-Order Cooks Night" before the Astros' game with the Padres in San Diego in 1974. So the Houston third baseman donned the chef's hat and apron, placed the lineup card in a big iron skillet, and headed out to home plate. He casually flipped the lineup card over like a hotcake when he reached the umpires.

The paid crowd of 12,000 fans—including 1,323 short-order cooks who entered the game free—applauded wildly even though they had been prepared to boo Rader.

Their anger at Rader stemmed from a misunderstanding over comments he made during the Astros' previous visit to San Diego a few months earlier. During a game, Padres owner Ray Kroc, the McDonald's hamburger king, had been so mad at his team that he commandeered the public address system and announced to the fans, "I have never seen such stupid ballplaying in my life!"

After the game, Rader told reporters, "Kroc must think he's dealing with a bunch of short-order cooks."

Chefs of fast-order establishments, who felt they had been put down by Rader, flooded him with complaints. "I never meant to demean somebody's occupation," Rader said in an apology. "What I said was a reflection on Kroc and nobody else."

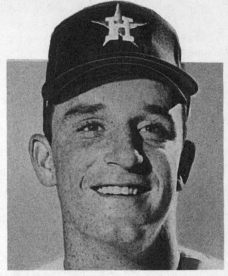

DOUG RADER cooked up fun.

When the Astros returned to San Diego, the enterprising Kroc declared it "Short-Order Cooks Night" and let the cooks in free.

Before the game, Rader decided to go along with the fun. He thought of wearing a sign on his back that said "Eat at Joe's" or "Eat at Burger King." But he settled on the chef's hat and apron and delivered the lineup card in a frying pan to the delight of the fans.

Once the game started, Padres fans continued to cheer Rader—at every mistake he made. They cheered when he struck out, when he was thrown out trying to stretch a single into a double, and when he made a fielding error.

Rader had a chance to shut them up when he came to bat with the bases loaded and two out in the ninth inning and Houston trailing 5-4. The cooks held their breath—then cheered lustily as Rader flied out to end the game.

Said Rader afterwards, "I didn't have much of a night out, but at least I pleased the cooks." ◇

Foul Ball Starts Fire — In Fan's Pocket!

...And Other Stories of Freaky Casualties

Crazed Groupie Shoots Phillies First Baseman!

In the most bizarre case of psychotic fan worship in major league history, a 19-year-old woman shot and nearly killed Philadelphia Phillies first baseman Eddie Waitkus.

Shortly after midnight on June 15, 1949, Waitkus received a note in his room at the Edgewater Beach Hotel in Chicago. The note, delivered by a hotel employee, was from a young woman who begged Waitkus to come to her room because of "something extremely important—it's extremely urgent that I see you as soon as possible."

Whether gallant or foolish, the single 29-year-old ballplayer went to her room and knocked on the door. It was opened by Ruth Ann Steinhagen, a Chicago stenographer, who invited him in and asked him to wait a second.

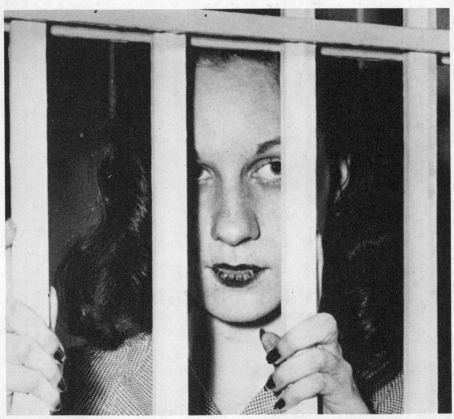

BEHIND BARS: Ruth Ann Steinhagen after shooting Eddie Waitkus.

She then walked over to a closet, pulled out a rifle, wheeled around, and said to the stunned Waitkus, "For two years you have been bothering me, and now you are going to die." Then she shot him in the chest.

The bullet punctured the player's lung, but he survived.

Waitkus had never met Steinhagen before the shooting. She had become infatuated with him two years earlier when she first saw him playing for the Chicago Cubs. Her secret obsession grew, but when Waitkus was traded to Philadelphia, she became deeply depressed and more fixated on him.

"I shot him because I liked him a great deal and I knew I couldn't have him," Steinhagen later said in a confession. "And if I couldn't have him, neither could anybody else." She was committed for psychiatric treatment.

Waitkus, who was batting .306 at the time of the shooting, missed the rest of the season. He returned in 1950 to help the Phillies win a pennant and was named Comeback Player of the Year. But even though he played six more years after the shooting, he never hit .300 again.

Some good did come out of the shooting. It inspired both a romance and a hit movie.

Waitkus fell in love with the nurse who was caring for him in the hospital and eventually married her.

And the incident formed the basis for the Bernard Malamud novel *The Natural,* which was turned into a movie of the same title. Robert Redford starred as talented rookie Roy Hobbs, who gets shot with a silver bullet by a mysterious woman in black in a Chicago hotel room. ◇

Catcher Loses Teeth in Attempt to Catch Ball Dropped From a Blimp

Cocky catcher Joe Sprinz thought he could snag a ball dropped from a dirigible 1,200 feet in the air. The result? He spit out a mouthful of teeth!

The stunt was dreamed up by promoters of the 1939 San Francisco World's Fair. They invited the city's minor league team, the San Francisco Seals, to try to catch a super "drop pitch." But the only one with the guts to try catching a ball thrown from a blimp was Sprinz, who later left his Pacific Coast team to play for the Cleveland Indians. He missed the first four balls that came hurtling out of the sky. They hit the ground with such tremendous force that they dug craters . . . but that didn't deter steel-nerved Sprinz from trying again.

"I saw the ball all the way, but it looked the size of an aspirin tablet," he later said.

Sprinz somehow got his mitt under the ball—but the monstrous impact slammed his gloved hand into his face, knocking him out cold.

When he woke up, Sprinz discovered he'd suffered a fractured jaw and severe cuts on both lips—and had spit out five choppers.

He missed a month of games, and probably would have given his eyeteeth not to have tried the tooth-losing stunt. ◇

During the 1940s, Bill Stockstick, groundskeeper at Sportsman's Park in St. Louis, had a special assistant to help him trim the outfield grass—his pet goat!

Bat Boy Almost Kills Babe Ruth —Later Portrays Him in Movie

In one of baseball's most ironic twists, a teenaged William Bendix was fired as a bat boy for almost killing Babe Ruth—and then grew up to star in a movie as the Bambino himself!

Bendix, famous for his TV role in "The Life of Riley," appeared in over 30 movies in his career. But acting wasn't Bendix's passion as a youth. Baseball was.

In 1922, at the age of 15, Bendix was lucky enough to become a bat boy for the New York Giants. In those days the New York Yankees shared the Polo Grounds with the Giants. Since Bendix had access to the clubhouse, he met his idol, the Babe, and quickly became his gofer. Ruth's every wish was Bendix's command. The star-

EX-BAT BOY WILLIAM BENDIX in a scene from "The Babe Ruth Story."

88

struck youth shined Babe's shoes, ran errands for him, and delivered food for the ever-hungry Sultan of Swat.

It was Bendix's eagerness to please his idol that caused the teenager to unwittingly nearly kill him.

One day before a game, Ruth sent Bendix off to fetch him a pregame snack of hot dogs and soft drinks. For Ruth, a snack was a dozen hot dogs and two quarts of soda. Bendix dutifully delivered the food, and Ruth, as usual, devoured all of it.

Right after the game, Ruth collapsed with stomach pains and was rushed to the hospital. Headlines across the country proclaimed that Ruth was seriously ill. Some even suggested he was dying. Actually, all he was suffering from was a bad case of indigestion.

Nevertheless, the Yankees' front office launched an immediate investigation into what had happened. Their conclusion: the bat boy was at fault for bringing the food to Ruth.

So the Giants fired Bendix.

Ruth quickly recovered, went on with his spectacular career, and soon forgot the hero-worshipping bat boy.

Meanwhile, the broken-hearted Bendix soured on baseball and turned his sights to acting. Twenty-six years later, in 1948, Bendix unintentionally again caused Ruth anguish. In the most notorious and widely-panned screen performance of his life, Bendix played the title role in *The Babe Ruth Story*. The movie was a box office flop.

A few months after its premiere, Ruth died. ◇

Foul Ball Starts a Fire—in Fan's Pocket

George Burns—the Detroit Tigers' first baseman, not the comedian—hit one of the most bizarre foul balls ever to land in the grandstand.

It started a fire in a fan's coat pocket!

The crazy incident occurred in August, 1915, when the Tigers were battling the Boston Red Sox for the pennant.

Burns came to bat against Boston in the seventh inning of a scoreless game and worked the count to 3-and-2 against Red Sox pitching star Dutch Leonard.

Burns fouled the next pitch into the grandstand. There was the usual flurry in the stands as some fans scattered to avoid the ball while others lunged for it.

On the next pitch, Leonard walked Burns. But before the batter reached first base, the commotion in the stands where his foul ball had previously landed flared up even more. "There's a man on fire here!" a fan yelled.

Looking up, the players could see a middle-aged man hopping up and down, with smoke coming out of the pocket of his sport coat.

A soft drink vendor raced to the rescue. He ran up to the fiery fan, opened a bottle of soda pop, and poured it into the man's pocket and squelched the fire.

Incredible as it sounds, the foul ball had hit the fan's coat and touched off a box of matches inside!

"It figures this would happen on a ball hit by a player named Burns," muttered the fan, who took off his scorched coat and stalked out of the ball park. ◇

★★★

Although Smith is the most common last name in the United States, there is nobody named Smith in the Baseball Hall of Fame.

Phillies Star Dreams of Chasing Fly Ball—Leaps Out of Window!

Sherry Magee—the star left fielder for the Philadelphia Phillies—was deep in sleep, dreaming of chasing a fly ball, when he leaped out of an open third-story window.

Miraculously, he survived without suffering any broken bones or internal injuries.

Magee, a sleepwalker, blamed his vivid dream on his bedtime snack—green grapes and ham sandwiches.

In its account of the bizarre incident on Sept. 14, 1908, *The Philadelphia Inquirer* reported:

"From a third-story window of the Junction Hotel, Magee, with a shriek that he was after a high flyer, jumped more than 12 feet to the roof of a stable below. Had the roof not stopped his fall, he would have been killed upon the stone pavement of the hotel yard.

"As it was, the player proved to be only slightly injured. The physicians at the German Hospital could not find a broken bone and, after an examination, sent Magee back to his hotel.

" 'I'll be back in the game in three or four days,' declared the ballplayer.

"Dr. John Boger says that the ballplayer has been working under mental strain for some time. He was completely absorbed in the race of the Phillies for the pennant, working like a beaver and wanting everybody else to do likewise. [Philadelphia finished fourth.]

"In an extremely nervous condition after a doubleheader, Magee aggravated matters before retiring in the evening by eating a bunch of green grapes and several ham sandwiches. As Magee himself said, 'Green grapes and ham sandwiches always do have a bad effect on me, but I thought I would take a chance.'

SHERRY MAGEE'S sleepwalking nearly killed him.

"The chance almost proved fatal. His wife, who was asleep in the same room, was awakened by excited cries from the ballplayer, 'Get together, come on . . . We've got 'em now.'

"Mrs. Magee went to procure some water. As she was returning with a pitcher, she saw her husband spring out of the bed with a wild leap and make for the window. She screamed and fell in her haste to catch Magee in time.

"The ballplayer was after a high flyer in his sleep. In his mind's eye, he saw it soaring just beyond the open window. With a frenzied leap and one arm raised high in the air, he jumped through the open window.

"Mrs. Magee stumbled over to the window and looked out. About 12 feet below, upon the roof of the stable, was the form of her husband in a heap. Everybody in the hotel was aroused. All expected to find the ballplayer dead or dying. 'Not a broken bone,' said the doctor. 'Just shaken up and bruised a bit.'

" 'It was one of the most exciting games I ever played, even though I was asleep,' Magee declared. 'I was going after a high flyer. Why, even when I jumped from the bed, I thought I was simply jumping a fence that seemed, somehow, to have grown up near left field on the Phillies' ground.

'I guess the grapes and ham sandwiches caused the trouble. They never did agree with me.' " ◊

Creepy Spider Nightmare Lands Toronto Player on DL

Toronto Blue Jays outfielder Glenallen Hill sleepwalked his way right onto the disabled list—after an horrific nightmare about spiders.

On the night of July 6, 1990, Hill—who suffers from arachnophobia, an extreme fear of spiders—went to bed in his home only to have a frighteningly realistic nightmare that huge, poisonous spiders were attacking him.

While still in his sleep, Hill bolted out of bed to fight off the spiders that were crawling everywhere in his mind—on the walls, the ceiling, the floors, and on him. Panic-stricken, Hill fled toward the stairway leading to the second floor. Unfortunately, he crashed into two glass coffee tables, smashing one of them.

So desperate was he to escape the spiders that Hill crawled on all fours right over sharp, broken shards of glass. When he finally woke up, he was relieved to discover that it was just a terrible dream. But he was also shocked to discover that he was bleeding from head to toe.

The broken glass lacerated his feet, arms, and elbows. His face was bruised and bleeding because he had smacked his head on a table during his blind rush to get away from the creepy crawlies.

Because of the cuts on his feet, Hill had to use crutches for a couple of

GLENALLEN HILL feared spiders.

days. In fact, he was so sliced up that the Blue Jays put him on the 15-day disabled list.

He managed to recover nicely from his sleepwalking injuries—but it took him a little longer to get over the ribbing he received from teammates and bench jockeys who kept calling him "Spider Man." ◊

Hurler Knocked Out by Lightning —But He Still Finishes Game!

Cleveland Indians pitcher Ray Caldwell was knocked down and out by a vicious bolt of lightning while on the mound. But amazingly, the hurler regained consciousness and, although somewhat dazed, finished the game—and won!

It was the only known time that a major leaguer has been hit by lightning during a game.

On August 24, 1919, the lanky righthander was twirling a nifty four-hitter against the Philadelphia Athletics and led 2-1 in the ninth inning at Cleveland's League Park.

He got the first two outs in the inning and was set to face batter Joe Dugan when, out of the blue, an horrific streak of lightning crashed near the mound, knocking Caldwell and several infielders off their feet.

"Thousands of spectators were thrown into momentary panic by the bolt which came without warning and made as much noise as the backfiring of a thousand autos or the explosion of a dozen shells from a battery of big Berthas," reported *The Cleveland Plain Dealer*. "Fully half of those in the stands were affected while every player felt the electrical current through his body, the spiked shoes they wore attracting the juice.

"Caldwell and shortstop [Ray] Chapman were affected the most. Caldwell lay stretched out on the pitching rubber, but he arose unassisted in a minute or so and the effects of the shock apparently wore off."

Indians manager Tris Speaker wanted to take Caldwell out of the game, but the pitcher refused. Although he was shaken by his close call with death, Caldwell stayed on the mound and then coaxed Dugan into grounding out to end the game.

RAY CALDWELL didn't let a bolt of lightning stop him from pitching.

Asked later what it was like to be struck by lightning, Caldwell said, "It felt like a sandbag hit me." He experienced no aftereffects from his lightning encounter and went on to win four of his next five games. ◇

Scooter Target of Death Threat...

Rizzuto, Martin Swap Jerseys —To Thwart a Mad Gunman!

New York Yankees star Phil Rizzuto gave Billy Martin the shirt off his back—so Martin could become the target for a madman instead of Rizzuto.

Manager Casey Stengel okayed the plan—because he felt he could afford to lose Martin more than he could risk losing Rizzuto.

After the Yankees clinched the pennant in 1950, they headed to Boston to play the Red Sox in the last three games of the season. Rizzuto, New York's scrappy shortstop, needed just one more hit to reach 200. "But I received a letter saying that if I played in Boston, I would be shot," recalled the Scooter.

Rizzuto took the letter seriously, and so did Stengel. However, Rizzuto, who would go on to win the American League's MVP award that season, really wanted that 200th hit, and was determined to play anyway. But he was definitely scared.

While the players were putting on their uniforms, rookie second baseman Billy Martin went up to the veteran Scooter and said, "Let's change uniforms. You wear my shirt and I'll wear yours. I'll take the chance and be the target. Besides, I can run faster than you."

Stengel thought that was a fine idea. "Billy was expendable," Rizzuto recalled with a laugh.

So the two infielders swapped numbers. Rizzuto donned teammate Billy's No. 1 while Martin wore Scooter's No. 10.

"The only thing I was worried about was that [Boston's hotheaded outfielder] Jimmy Piersall would take a swing at me, thinking I was Billy," said Rizzuto. "He and Billy were always fighting."

Rizzuto didn't stay on the field very long. He singled in the first inning for his 200th hit and was immediately lifted from the game. Martin, meanwhile, had to finish the game wearing Phil's number. "Poor Billy. He didn't stand still the whole game," said Rizzuto.

Fortunately for everyone, the man with the gun never did carry out his threat to shoot Rizzuto. ◇

★ ★ ★

World Series Losers Make More Money Than Winners

The Boston Red Sox whipped the Pittsburgh Pirates five games to three in the 1903 World Series—yet the losing players received more money than the winners!

Each member on the Red Sox earned $1,182, while each player on the defeated Pirates walked away with $1,316—$134 more. That's because Pirates owner Barney Dreyfuss generously threw the club's share of the Series profits into the players' pool, to be divided evenly among them. But tight-fisted Red Sox owner Henry Killilea pocketed his share of Boston's profits, $6,699.56.

It just didn't pay for the Red Sox to win.

She Was Cheering Son on Mother's Day...
Feller's Pitch Fouled Off His Mom's Face!

Mother's Day, 1939 was both a memorable and painful day for Lena Feller, mom of Cleveland Indians superstar hurler Bob Feller. While watching her son pitch, she was struck by a vicious line drive foul that injured her so badly she was rushed to the hospital.

Feller's family had journeyed from their home in Van Meter, Iowa, to Chicago to watch Rapid Robert pitch against the White Sox at Comiskey Park. Feller had arranged for his folks to sit in box seats on the first base side close to the field so he could see them from the mound.

He set the White Sox down in order in the first two innings and was cruising along with a 6-0 lead when the near-tragedy occurred in the third inning.

Chicago pinch hitter Marvin Owen

BOB FELLER and his mother at home before the near-tragic accident.

lashed a wicked foul ball into the stands. And out of 30,000 people, the ball hit Mrs. Feller in the face just above her right eye. The impact broke the poor lady's glasses and opened up a deep cut.

Feller rushed to the stands to check on his mother, who was hurt and bleeding but still conscious. "I felt sick," Feller later recalled. "I saw the police and ushers leading her out of the stands so they could take her to the hospital . . . There wasn't anything I could do, so I went on pitching."

But he was so shaken up that he lost his control, walked several batters, and gave up three runs in the inning.

However, he settled down and finished the game, winning it 9-4. Then he rushed to the hospital where his mom had been given six stitches. She was put under observation for two days.

"Mother looked up from the hospital bed, her face bruised and both eyes blackened, and she was still able to smile reassuringly," Feller recalled. "She told me, 'My head aches, Robert, but I'm all right. Now don't go blaming yourself. It wasn't your fault.'

"It was a one-in-a-million shot that my mother, while sitting in a crowd, would be struck by a foul ball resulting from a pitch I had made."

And on Mother's Day, no less. ◇

INSULTING INJURIES

Ballplayers can get hurt in the strangest ways—even when they are far away from the ball park. Here are some examples:

• Pittsburgh Pirates relief pitcher Brian Fisher sustained a 13-inch gash on his left arm while playing miniature golf! In 1989, he was leaning on his golf club when it snapped in two and sliced his arm.

• Texas Rangers hurler Charlie Hough fractured the little finger on his pitching hand in 1986 when he shook hands with a friend.

• New York Mets pitcher Bobby Ojeda cut off the tip of the middle finger of his pitching hand while clipping hedges at his home in 1988.

• In 1989, New York Yankees pitcher Dave Eiland missed several appearances in spring training after cutting a finger on his pitching hand trying to open a crab claw at dinner.

• In 1969, Atlanta Braves hurler Cecil Upshaw was walking along the sidewalk when he decided to show his teammates how he could dunk an imaginary basketball by leaping high and slapping an awning. But his ring got caught and tore up his finger so badly he needed over three hours of micro-surgery.

• White Sox outfielder Carlos May blew half his thumb off with a mortar during National Guard summer camp in 1969.

• Chicago Cubs pitcher Bobo Newsom had just recovered from a broken leg suffered in a car accident in 1932 when he visited a mule auction. A mule reared back, kicked him, and broke his same leg again!

• Chicago Cubs pitcher Dizzy Dean was being driven home from Wrigley Field by teammate Rip Russell in 1940 when the passenger-side door suddenly swung open. Dean fell out and bounced his head on the road. Aside from cuts and bruises, Dizzy was all right, adding with tongue in cheek, "There's not much upstairs that can break anyway."

A Polo Grounds Whodunit...

MURDER IN THE GRANDSTAND

A New York Giants fan was shot to death as he sat in the grandstand watching batting practice before a July 4, 1950 doubleheader with the Brooklyn Dodgers.

And to this day, nobody knows where the bullet came from . . . or who fired the shot.

The victim, Bernard Doyle, 54, a former boxing manager, was sitting in the upper deck of the Polo Grounds between left and center field. He had brought along Otto Flaig, Jr., the freckle-faced 13-year-old son of a friend. Doyle, with scorecard in hand, had just turned to Otto to make a remark when the boy and the fans next to the pair heard a loud "pop."

As 40,000 spectators watched the action on the field, a single .22 caliber slug from out of nowhere crashed into Doyle's head just above the left temple. He never knew what hit him.

A doctor rushed to the victim's side, but there was nothing the physician could do. He pronounced Doyle dead at the scene.

Working on the theory that the shot had been fired from outside the ball park, police scoured the rooftops of Coogan's Bluff and found empty shells from a .22 on the roof of a building 750 feet from the spot where Doyle was killed. (A .22 caliber bullet has a range of 1,500 feet.)

A 14-year-old teenager who lived in the building and owned two .22 caliber rifles was taken into custody for questioning but later released.

Police never did find the killer and today the case remains one of baseball's most baffling unsolved mysteries. ◇

★ ★ ★

Umpire Hit 7 Times by Balls During Game

American League umpire Steve Palermo had a hot date with Ben-Gay after a Seattle Mariners-Kansas City Royals game on Sept. 17, 1990. The plate umpire was left battered and bruised by seven balls that caromed off his body.

Mariners hurler Russ Swan and Royals pitcher Chris Codiroli combined for three wild pitches that bounded off the front of the plate and smacked into Palermo.

The umpire was nailed on the right foot, left hand, and left shin from the errant tosses. After Codiroli's second wild pitch, recalled Palmero, "Codiroli told me he wasn't trying to hit me on purpose. I told him he'd better not or I'd throw him out."

It obviously wasn't Palmero's day. When he wasn't getting nicked by wild pitches, he was getting banged up by batters.

Four times foul tips slammed into the unlucky arbiter.

After the final out was made, Palmero hobbled off the field to the dressing room where he showed his fellow umps souvenirs of the game— seven black and blue bruises.

Foul Ball Causes Cannery Explosion...
Boston Backers Bombarded by Baked Beans!

Boston Red Sox fans were pelted by a shower of boiling hot baked beans following an explosion at Boston's biggest bean cannery.

And it all happened because of a foul ball.

On August 11, 1903, the visiting Philadelphia Athletics were playing the Boston Red Sox at the Huntington Avenue Grounds. In the seventh inning, A's pitcher Rube Waddell blasted a long foul over the right field bleachers that landed on the roof of the biggest bean cannery in Boston.

According to the game account in the *Philadelphia North American,* "The ball jammed itself between the steam whistle and the stem of the valve that operates it. The pressure set the whistle blowing."

Although it was about 4:50 p.m., many cannery workers assumed the whistle meant it was quitting time, so they started to leave the building.

"The incessant screeching of the bean-factory whistle led engineers in neighboring factories to think fire had broken out and they turned on their whistles," said the newspaper. "With a dozen whistles going full blast, a policeman sent in an alarm of fire."

By now, everyone in the cannery had fled the building, leaving unattended a huge steaming cauldron bubbling with a ton of beans. Just as the fire wagons arrived, the cauldron blew up.

"A shower of scalding beans descended on the bleachers and caused a small panic," said the report. "One man went insane. When he saw the beans dropping out of a cloud of steam, the unfortunate rooter yelled, 'The end of the world is coming and we will all be destroyed!' An ambulance . . . conveyed the demented man to his home. The ton of beans proved a total loss."

The blast of beans had one positive effect though. It dislodged the foul ball and finally stopped the annoying whistle from blowing. ◇

A Patriotic Catch!

St. Louis Cardinal infielder Keith Hernandez catches a flying flag that floated to the ground during a fireworks display at a 1980 game.

Field of NIGHTMARES

Freaky injuries to ballplayers occur everywhere—in the clubhouse and dugout, during batting practice, and even while walking to the on-deck circle. For example:

• Oakland A's catcher Mickey Tettleton was placed on the disabled list in 1987 with a foot infection—caused by tying his shoelaces too tight!

• The Texas Rangers' Darrell Porter tripped and fell in the on-deck circle in a 1986 game against the Chicago White Sox and fractured his left ankle.

• Infielder Lonnie Frey was standing in the Cincinnati Reds' dugout in 1940 when the lid to the water cooler slipped off and fell on him—breaking a bone in his right foot.

• On Opening Day, 1946, Washington Senators infielder George Myatt leaped from the dugout to rush onto the field in the first inning. But he tripped and sprawled backwards—and broke his ankle.

• During batting practice in 1949, Chicago Cubs third baseman Andy Pafko muffed a ground ball, then stumbled over it as he tried to pick it up—and sprained his ankle. He was out of action for a week.

• One of the freakiest pregame injuries occurred to St. Louis Cardinals outfielder Vince Coleman during the 1985 National League Championship Series. Coleman was standing on a tarp casually warming up at Busch Stadium when an operator activated the automatic rolling machine. The tarp started to roll out with Coleman's foot still in it. Unfortunately, the outfielder's foot and leg were so badly bruised that he missed the rest of the playoffs and the entire World Series. ◇

★★★

Game Is Sunned Out!

A college baseball game was actually called because of too much sun!

It happened in May, 1976 when Colgate was playing St. Lawrence College in Canton, New York. It was a cloudless, beautiful spring day, perfect for baseball—for a while.

As the late afternoon sun began its descent, Old Sol remained uncommonly strong and bright. By the time the game went into extra innings, the low sun was shining directly into the eyes of the hitter, catcher, and plate umpire.

Umpire Arnold Dunn let the game proceed into the eleventh inning before he decided he had seen, or rather not seen, enough. He called the game with the score tied 1-1.

"This game is sunned out!" he declared. "By the time we will be able to see the ball again, the sun will have set and it will be too dark to play." (The ball park did not have any lights.)

And so, for the only time in baseball history, a game was called because the sun was shining too brightly.

Nervous Runner Turns Homer Into Double Play!

...And Other Startling Baserunning Stories

Mutt Appears in Box Score —After Running the Bases!

A little yellow mongrel holds a unique spot in basball history. He is the only dog to ever appear in a box score.

The pooch had been adopted by Roberto Ortiz, a new member of the Charlotte Hornets of the Piedmont League. Ortiz arrived in Charlotte, North Carolina, from Cuba in 1941 as a hot prospect for the Washington Senators.

Because he could barely speak English at first, Ortiz felt lonely in Charlotte and soon befriended the mutt that hung around the local stadium.

Ortiz named the pooch Yellow Dog. Every day, the mongrel tagged along as Ortiz walked to a local restaurant for dinner. Yellow Dog waited outside until Ortiz finished his meal and then fed him the leftovers. At night, Ortiz bunked in a little apartment beneath the left field bleachers while Yellow Dog slept by the door.

When the team worked out, the mutt romped alongside Ortiz. Each day, when Ortiz completed batting practice, he raced around the bases and Yellow Dog—with his ears flopping in the wind—ran along with him. Ortiz taught the mongrel not only to touch each base but also to go into a slide by rolling over at full speed. The canine slide cracked up everyone who saw it.

General manager Phil Howser liked to watch Yellow Dog run the bases, too—but only during pregame practice. Howser told Ortiz that during games the dog had to be locked up in his apartment on the other side of the fence. But during a 1941 game against Norfolk, Yellow Dog made baseball history.

Ortiz apparently had left the apartment door open. So after a nap, the mutt ambled along the foul line toward the dugout.

It was the bottom of the ninth inning and Charlotte was down by a run when the first batter walked and Ortiz came

ROBERTO ORTIZ ran the bases with his dog right behind him.

to the plate. He then socked a ball that crashed into the center field wall. Ortiz was steaming around first base when a yellow blur joined him. It was Yellow Dog scampering at his master's heels. Down to second base they went, but they didn't stop there. As Ortiz neared third, he hit the dirt . . . and so did Yellow Dog.

The fans and umpire stared in disbelief as Yellow Dog curled up into a rolling slide, arriving just behind Ortiz.

The umpire peered into a cloud of dust and gave the safe signal twice, first for Ortiz and then for the pooch. The fans roared with laughter. Ortiz got up, dusted himself off, then handed Yellow Dog to the team trainer.

Up in the press box, the official scorer pondered for a moment, then made his historic decision. The next day, the *Charlotte News* ran its box score for the game. Right under Ortiz's name, it read: "y— Yellow Dog." Down below in the box score, in the space reserved for pinch runners and pinch hitters, this notation appeared: "y— Yellow Dog ran with Ortiz in the 9th." ◇

Nervous Runner Turns Home Run Into Double Play

Minor leaguer Hargis Sugar was such a nervous wreck that in his professional debut, he forgot how to run the bases—and wound up turning a home run into a double play!

Hargis was a talented amateur player who was finally convinced to sign with a professional team in Waco, Texas, in 1888. A real country boy who was very shy, Hargis turned pro only after his friends urged him to put his talents on display for pay. So he reported to Waco and was immediately inserted into the lineup as the team's new right fielder.

As Hargis stepped up to the plate for the first time, he gazed at the 800 people in the stands—a huge crowd by 1888 standards—and his nerves just shattered. He had never seen that many people before in one place. Heck, he had never even been away from home before.

Hargis was so jittery at the plate that he literally jumped around in the batter's box. The pitcher had a tough time telling where Hargis' strike zone was and walked him. Hargis, still in a nervous daze, somehow managed to wobble down to first base. The next batter, Harry Taylor, then blasted a shot over the fence and began his home run trot.

Hargis took off at the crack of the bat—but not to second base. Instead, for some bizarre reason, the Nervous Nelly raced to right field, then center field, then left field, and finally slid into third base, apparently thinking it was home plate!

Taylor, meanwhile, had continued trotting around the bases with his head down, assuming that the rookie runner was well in front of him. Taylor had touched third and was on his way to home by the time the wayward Hargis dashed in from left field and slid into third.

When Taylor reached the plate, he was astonished to see the umpire call him out for passing a runner on base. The ump then pointed to the frazzled Hargis at third, and called him out, too—for running out of the baselines.

So, for the only time in the long history of baseball, a home run resulted in a double play! ◇

Giants Player Duels Horse In Crazy Race Around Bases

In the most bizarre baserunning ever seen on a baseball diamond, New York Giants infielder Hans Lobert raced against a horse!

It happened during spring training in 1915 in Oxnard, California, where Giants manager John McGraw challenged a jockey to race his steed against the speedy Lobert.

"The horse was supposed to race along a line just outside the bases and I was to touch the bags on the inside corner," recalled Lobert. "I was to run just the same as if I were trying for an inside-the-park homer.

"We took off from home plate together. I really got going and I must have been a dozen feet in front going down to second when the jockey swerved the horse over, trying to cut across the bag. He darn near rode me down.

"It cost me ground and by the time we reached third, that horse was breathing down the back of my neck. Then we cut for home and the jockey used the spurs and whip and we raced over the plate hell-bent for leather.

"[Umpire] Bill Klem was the judge for the race. I went up to him all out of breath and ready to collapse and said, 'I won the race, didn't I?' Bill gave me a look and bellowed, 'The horse wins by a nose!'

"I shook my fist in Klem's face and yelled, 'Look at this beak of mine. Look at the size of my schnozzle. No horse in this world could beat me by a nose.' But Klem's decision stuck.

"McGraw was laughing a fit. He said he was going to enter me in the Kentucky Derby." ◇

HANS LOBERT never quit jabbering about his zany horse race.

Acrobatic Player Somersaults Over First Baseman for Single!

In the strangest baserunning in World Series history, the St. Louis Browns' Arlie Latham somersaulted his way to first.

It happened during the fourth game of the 1885 Series between St. Louis of the American Association and the Chicago White Stockings (forerunners of the Cubs) of the National League.

In the bottom of the eighth inning, the Browns were at bat trailing 2-1. With one out, Latham stepped to the plate and laid a bunt down the first base line. Chicago player-manager Cap Anson charged in from his first base position, scooped up the ball, and stood ready to tag Arlie as he ran toward the bag.

Latham dashed to within a yard of Anson, and the out seemed assured. But then, at the last possible second, Arlie suddenly launched himself head over heels in the air. He turned a perfect midair somersault right over Anson's glove, and landed safely on first base.

Anson was so stunned by the move that he never even made a swipe at Arlie as he went flying overhead. Worse yet for Chicago, Latham's tumbling act triggered a Browns rally. Arlie eventually scored the tying run, and St. Louis pushed across another tally in the inning to win 3-2.

The Series ended in a tie. Each team won three games and tied once (the first game was called by darkness with the score knotted 5-5). Thanks to Latham's somersault, St. Louis shared the world championship. ◇

★★★

Ump Delays Game Until Tardy Rookie Arrives

Umpire Ollie Chill held up the start of a Washington Senators game on Sept. 20, 1915, because one player—a rookie, no less—hadn't shown up yet.

But the fans didn't utter a single complaint because the missing man was Joe Judge, a first baseman being hailed as the most sensational new player in years. He had just led Buffalo, of the International League, to the pennant. When the press announced that the Senators had called Judge up to the bigs and would play in his first major league game, fans flocked to the ball park just to see him.

But by game time, Judge had yet to arrive because the train from Buffalo to Washington was late, although it had just arrived at the station.

Since the umpire didn't want a ball park full of disappointed fans, he held up the start of the 3 p.m. game while everyone waited for the rookie. Finally, here came the Judge. He frantically ran into the clubhouse, threw on a uniform, and grabbed his glove. At 3:20 p.m. he raced to first base without a chance to limber up.

Judge was spectacular that day, knocking in two runs and catching everything but a cold. He went on to play 20 years in the bigs, mostly with the Senators, and wound up with a lifetime batting average of .298. Judge had proven that all good things really do come to those who wait. ◇

Phils Hit Into DP—And No Fielders Touched the Ball

The Philadelphia Phillies were victimized by a bizarre double play in which no fielders touched the ball.

In the top of the seventh inning of an 1889 game between the visiting Phils and the Chicago Cubs, Philadelphia put runners Billy Hallman on third and Jack Clements on second with no outs.

Batter Ben Sanders then whacked a hard line drive down the third base line. As the ball headed straight for him, Hallman froze, not knowing which way to go. Clements, meanwhile, who had taken a good lead off second, dashed toward third at the crack of the bat.

The ball struck Hallman on the shoulder. But instead of falling to the ground, the ball caromed crazily into the third base path . . . and then hit the oncharging Clements!

The umpire ruled both men were out because they were each hit by a batted ball.

The Phillies howled in protest, arguing only Hallman should be out because the ball was dead after it hit him. But the umpire pointed out that since the ball had never been touched by a defensive player, it was still considered a batted ball after striking Hallman. Therefore, Clements was out, too. ◇

Fan Falls Hard for Ballgirl

An unidentified fan falls out of his seat and onto the field as he tries to talk ballgirl Cindy Crawford into giving him the foul ball she retrieved during a 1980 night game in Texas between the Red Sox and Rangers.

Runner Steals Home—And He Didn't Know It

Pittsburgh Pirates player-manager Fred Clarke made the most unusual steal of home plate in baseball history—because he didn't even know he was swiping it at the time.

During a 1906 game against the Chicago Cubs, the Pirates loaded the bases with Clarke on third. On a 3-and-1 pitch to batter Jim Nealon, Cubs hurler Three Finger Brown zipped the ball across the plate about letter-high.

Home plate umpire Hank O'Day didn't utter a word. Since the ump remained silent, Clarke assumed it was a ball and casually trotted down the line.

When Nealon saw Clarke ambling home, he assumed it was ball four also, so he flipped his bat and ran down to first. O'Day's silence convinced Cubs catcher Johnny Kling that it was a walk, so he tossed the ball back to the mound.

But just as Clarke casually touched home plate, O'Day suddenly shouted, "Strike two!" Everyone froze, turned, and stared at the umpire.

"There was a frog in my throat," the embarrassed O'Day explained. "I couldn't say a word."

Now that he could speak and make his call, the ump summoned Nealon back to the batter's box with a full count. But because time had not been called and Clarke had advanced to home at his own risk, the run counted. Not until after he had returned to the dugout did Clarke realize he had stolen home. ◇

★★★

White Sox, Giants Play In Shadow of Pyramid

Major leaguers played in the most imposing shadow ever in baseball history—cast by the Great Pyramid in Egypt.

In 1914, the New York Giants and Chicago White Sox played to a 3-3 tie in an exhibition game at the base of the Great Pyramid. It was all part of an offseason 56-game world tour to promote baseball.

The teams visited such cities as Shanghai, Hong Kong, Manila, Rome, and Nice.

A Free Plug for His Boss' TV Station!

When Atlanta Braves owner Ted Turner signed Andy Messersmith in 1976, Turner—owner of then superstation Channel 17—had this special uniform ready for him. But, the league banned it.

Phils Victim of a Triple Play —And No Ball Was Ever Hit!

On May 21, 1950, Eddie Waitkus of the Philadelphia Phillies "hit" into a trio of outs against the St. Louis Cardinals—and he didn't even take the bat off his shoulder.

With runners Richie Ashburn on second base and Granny Hamner at first, Waitkus took a called third strike. Meanwhile, Ashburn had broken for third, so Cardinals catcher Joe Garagiola snapped the ball to third baseman Tommy Glaviano. Ashburn quickly put on the brakes, but found himself caught in a rundown. Shortstop Marty Marion then tagged him for out number two.

By this time, Hamner had strayed too far off first base, so Marion flung the ball to first baseman Stan Musial who tagged Hamner for the final out of the triple play.

Thirty-two years later, the New York Yankees also were victimized by a hitless triple play.

On May 29, 1982, in a game against the Minnesota Twins, New York had runners Bobby Murcer on second and Graig Nettles on first and no outs. With a full count on batter Roy Smalley, both runners took off on the next pitch.

But Smalley struck out. Murcer skidded to a stop halfway to third and hustled back toward second. Meanwhile, Nettles, who had reached second, made a U-turn and raced back toward first.

Twins catcher Sal Butera picked off Nettles with a hard throw to first baseman Kent Hrbek. Then, for reasons known only to himself, Murcer took off for third base—again.

But Hrbek's throw to pitcher Terry Felton, who was covering third on the play, nailed Murcer for the third out in a hitless—and witless—triple play. ◇

Squeeze Play

During a 1973 game between players and wives, the Minnesota Twins' Danny Walton tries to squeeze out a joke by wearing a girdle—and this wacky sign.

Booing Philly Fans Drive Dodgers Pitcher From Mound!

...And Other Outrageous Fan Stories

1,115 Grandstand Skippers...

Fans Manage Browns For a Day—And Win!

Proving that more than 1,000 heads are better than one, Bill Veeck, the outrageous owner of the St. Louis Browns, turned his club over to the fans to manage for one game.

And, remarkably, the grandstand managers showed an uncanny ability to make the right moves—and guided the Browns to a history-making 5-3 win.

On August 24, 1951, in a home game against the seventh-place Philadelphia Athletics, the cellar-dwelling Browns put their fate in the hands of the "Grandstand Managers Club." Fans qualified for membership by sending the team proposed batting orders.

All 1,115 grandstand managers were squeezed into seats behind the home dugout. They were given large white signs with "YES" in red on one side and "NO" in green on the other. They were told to flash one side or the other in

GRANDSTAND MANAGERS disagree over what play to call.

response to questions of strategy, posed on placards by the Browns' coaches. Majority ruled.

Meanwhile, the club's real manager, Zack Taylor, sat in a rocking chair in a third-base box seat, smoking a pipe and wearing a white shirt, slacks, and bedroom slippers.

The Athletics weren't too thrilled with Veeck's latest promotion. The A's front office blasted Veeck for making "a travesty of the game." A's skipper Jimmy Dykes warned he would protest the game if the grandstand managers caused any delays. While it may have appeared time-consuming for the fans to decide, the game was played in a brisk 2 hours and 11 minutes.

But the real surprise of the night was that the fans proved they could make the right moves.

The first decision they made was to reject the lineup submitted by the club's coaches. The fans benched catcher Matt Batts and rookie first baseman Ben Taylor and replaced them, respectively, with Sherm Lollar and Hank "Bow Wow" Arft. Incredibly, Lollar and Arft were the batting stars of the game, combining for four hits, four RBI, and three runs.

It was just the first of many good moves by the "managers." They were faced with two critical decisions in the first inning—and were proven right both times.

Browns pitcher Ned Garver got off to a rocky start, allowing five of the first six batters to get on base safely. When the A's Gus Zernial blasted a three-run homer, the fans were asked, "Shall we warm up a pitcher?"

"No," the majority decided. Garver rewarded their faith by giving up only two hits the rest of the game.

Also in the first frame, with A's runners on first and third and one out, the fans were asked if the infield should play back for the double play at the risk of giving up a run if it failed. "Yes," they voted. The next batter then grounded into an inning-ending twin killing.

Later, the grandstand managers voted "no" to running Lollar from first on a 3-and-2 pitch with one out. It was a good thing they did because the batter struck out and the slow-footed Lollar would have been easily nailed at second. Instead, he eventually scored the tying run on back-to-back hits.

The fans made only one wrong decision the entire game—when they sent Arft to steal second base and he was caught. (Perhaps that's because the A's couldn't help but steal the sign.)

After the final out was made and the victorious Browns trotted off the field, the grandstand managers were thanked with a fireworks display that said: "THANK YOU, G.S. MANAGERS, FOR A SWELL JOB."

Zack Taylor, who returned to the dugout as manager the next day, said he learned something from the fans. "They seemed to be divided about 60-40 on every call. Now they know what we managers go through. That's why we have gray hair." ◊

Ty Cobb's Number Never Retired

The uniform number of Detroit Tigers Hall of Famer Ty Cobb was never retired.

Even though he won 12 batting titles during his career and retired with a .367 lifetime batting average—the best ever in the major leagues—the Tigers never retired his number.

That's because he never wore one. Cobb's playing days ended in 1926, three years before players regularly wore numbers on their backs.

Fan Sues Giants for the Right to Keep a Foul Ball

Fans have a right to keep what has become the game's most cherished souvenir—a ball hit into the stands—thanks to a spectator who sued the New York Giants over a foul ball.

On May 16, 1921, Reuben Berman was sitting with friends in box seats at the Polo Grounds, watching the Giants play the Cincinnati Reds.

In the middle of the game, a batter popped a foul ball into the stands. Reuben leaped out of his seat and caught the ball on the fly. He and his friends delighted in the catch and marveled over the ball, which seconds earlier had been the object of everyone's attention in the park.

But back then, teams like the Giants made it a practice to retrieve as many foul balls from the stands as possible to save money.

Within a few minutes, a burly usher approached Reuben's section and demanded the return of the ball. Reuben refused to throw the ball to the usher, who then proceeded to move down the row toward the defiant fan. In protest, Rueben tossed the ball behind him and watched it disappear into a crowd of fans scrambling for the ball park prize.

The angry usher then unceremoniously removed Reuben from his seat and took him to the Giants' executive offices.

There he was scolded for not returning the ball, handed a refund on his ticket, and escorted out of the park.

It could have ended there. But Reuben Berman was angry. He felt humiliated and embarrassed over his treatment and he wanted justice. So he sued the Giants' owners for $20,000 for mental and bodily distress over being thrown out of the Polo Grounds.

The case went to trial where a jury ruled in Reuben's favor, but awarded him only $100.

However, fans everywhere were the big winners. Because of Reuben's lawsuit, the Giants dropped their policy of demanding the return of foul balls, and soon other teams did, too.

Now, under "Reuben's Rule," any baseball hit into the stands can be kept by any fan who is lucky enough to catch it.

★★★

Outfielder Plays on Both Teams—In Same Game!

Minor leaguer Mark Davidson actually played outfield for both teams in the same inning!

Davidson started in right field for the Portland Beavers in a 1989 Pacific Coast League game against the Tucson Toros. After the top of the first inning, the game was suspended, rather than postponed, and resumed three weeks later.

In the meantime, Davidson was traded by Portland's parent club, the Minnesota Twins, to the Houston Astros, who assigned him to Tucson. When the suspended game was resumed in the bottom of the first inning, Davidson was again in the outfield—only this time in left field in a Toros' uniform!

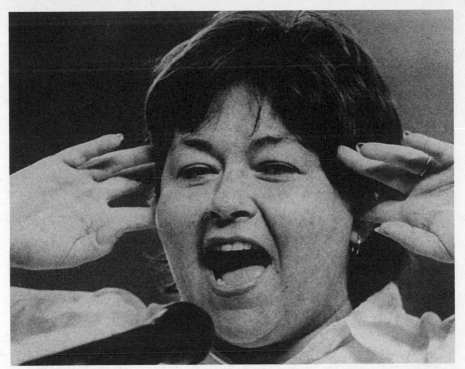

ROSEANNE BARR screeches her rendition of the national anthem.

Roseanne Target of Death Threats For Butchering National Anthem!

Comedienne Roseanne Barr was the victim of dozens of death threats when she outraged America by lousing up the revered national anthem before a San Diego Padres game at Jack Murphy Stadium in 1990.

Roseanne turned the crowd of 25,744 into a howling mob with her shrill, off-key rendition of the anthem. The booing increased to a fever pitch when she finished her screeching by spitting on the ground, grabbing her crotch, and then walking off the field with a laugh.

After seeing her star-spangled boner on TV, thousands of furious fans phoned television and radio stations to blast Roseanne for her shameful actions. Even President Bush called her performance a "disgrace."

Some incensed people got so carried away that 40 death threats were phoned into the producers of Roseanne's TV show. Although the threats were nothing more than angry words, one furious fan threw a "bomb" made of Roman candles on the porch of the star's Malibu home. Nearby was a chilling note: "Next time it won't be just fireworks."

Roseanne's producers were so worried about her safety that they tightened security on the set by bringing in bomb-sniffing dogs. The mutts checked the set for explosives every morning and every night, but never found anything.

Roseanne confessed to friends that she had no idea how upset America would be over her singing. At first she thought it was funny. As she walked off the field, reporters asked for a comment about the fans who had begun booing her right after her ear-rattling opening lines. In her own flippant style, Roseanne responded, "The boos? Yeah, well, it was just because those people weren't sitting up front to hear my wonderful singing."

Echoing the opinions of his team-mates, Padres pitcher Eric Show declared, "It was a total embarrassment to the club. What a mistake. It's an insult to the song and all the people who died for what we have left of freedom."

An Associated Press account described Roseanne's singing as "crude, even lewd, but this time fans were spared seeing where she's tattooed." That was a reference to her antics at a 1989 World Series game in Oakland when she mooned fans and revealed a "Tom" tattoo in honor of her husband Tom Arnold. ◇

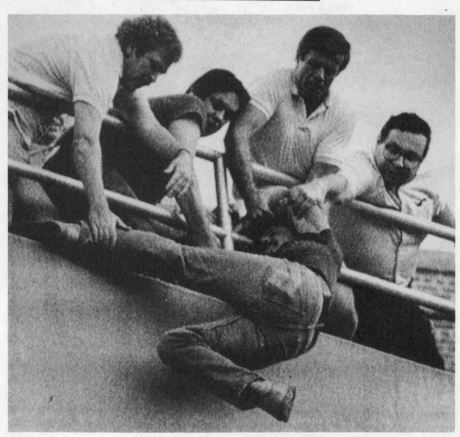

Fan Falls for Foul Fly

A fan is helped up over the upper deck railing after he fell over while trying to catch a foul ball during a game between Kansas City and the Orioles at Baltimore in 1958. The fan was treated for a cut lip.

Cop Robs Cubs of Extra-Base Hit

A member of Chicago's mounted police enraged the Cubs by robbing them of an extra-base hit in a pivotal play that cost the team a victory.

Moments before the 1936 game with the visiting Brooklyn Dodgers at Wrigley Field, the cop took a seat on the bench in the Dodgers' bullpen located in foul territory 100 feet past first base. He quickly dozed off only to be awakened by the roar of the crowd in the first inning. Cubs batter Phil Cavarretta had slashed a drive that went inside first base by two feet and then bounded toward the Dodgers' bullpen.

As he opened his eyes, the policeman saw the ball heading right toward him. Acting as though he were wearing a Dodgers uniform rather than that of Chicago's finest, the cop fielded the ball and threw it to Brooklyn right fielder Randy Moore. By that time, Cavarretta was pulling into third base. But because Moore had the ball, the runner decided against trying for home. The Cub baserunner seemed satisfied with a triple.

But plate umpire Charley Moran ordered Cavarretta to go back all the

...and steals game from Chicago!

way to first base because of the policeman's interference on the play. The next two batters grounded out, ending the inning without a run scoring.

The fans were so outraged by the cop's action that he quickly walked out of Wrigley Field, hopped on his horse, and rode away.

The policeman's play turned out to be the crucial one of the game. He prevented Cavarretta from getting a triple, a possible inside-the-park home run, or, at the very least, a chance to score.

One run would have won it for the Cubs because the two teams went into extra innings tied 0—0. The Dodgers pushed across a tally in the tenth to win 1-0 . . . and they owed it all to a game-stealing cop. ◇

Errors Cheaper by the Dozen

The Detroit Tigers and Chicago White Sox each played a game as though errors were cheaper by the dozen.

The Tigers committed a record 12 muffs in a game against Chicago on May 1, 1901, prompting *The Detroit Free Press* to say, "Never has a team representing Detroit ever played such a miserable game." The Tigers fumbled, bumbled, and stumbled their way to a 19-9 drubbing.

Two years later, on May 6, 1903, the White Sox returned the favor, mishandling 12 balls against Detroit. This time *The Chicago Tribune* called it "the craziest game that ever disgraced a major league diamond." The fielding miscues by the Sox "would have been a discredit to a high school nine," the paper aded.

Despite the dirty dozen errors, the White Sox still managed to win 10-9.

Philly Fans Boo Dodgers Pitcher Off the Mound!

Los Angeles Dodgers pitcher Burt Hooton was hooted off the mound by Philadelphia Phillies fans in the third game of the 1977 National League Championship Series.

Staked to a 2-0 lead, Hooton was struggling in the bottom of the second inning at Veterans Stadium. With two men on base and two out, Hooton had a 1-and-2 count on Phillies hurler Larry Christenson. Hooton then reared back and fired what he believed was an inning-ending strike three. But plate umpire Harry Wendelstedt called it a ball.

"I turned and kicked the rubber real hard," Hooton recalled. "Everybody seemed to be watching. A few fans started yelling, then more picked it up and it just started to go around. It got noisier than those jets at Shea Stadium except it went on and on with every pitch. I lost my cool."

Hooton was so rattled that he walked Christenson to load the bases. Then as the crescendo of hoots from 63,000 Philly fans intensified, the flustered hurler walked the next three batters before he was taken out of the game (which the Dodgers won 6-5).

"I lost my composure and never got it back," Hooton admitted.

"The noise from those fans was unbelievable." ◇

BURT HOOTON throws his hands up in disgust as the fans boo.

114

Fan Declares Himself Free Agent, Signs 'Contract' With Other Team

A Chicago Cubs fan became so upset with his club that he declared himself a "free agent" who was available to the highest bidder. After ten teams expressed interest in him, he switched his allegiance—to a minor league team.

On Jan. 3, 1977, TV cameraman Alan Hartwick, of Grand Rapids, Michigan, sent a letter to every major league team—except the Cubs—announcing that he was becoming America's first free agent fan.

"I have been a Chicago Cubs fan for 20 years," he wrote. "Whether the score has been Pittsburgh 22, Chicago 0, or Pittsburgh 22, Chicago 1, I have stuck with the Cubs to the end. But I don't have a contract with the Cubs' organization. All the Cubs have given me over the years have been a couple of season schedules and games postponed because of darkness. At this moment, I am a fan without a team. I will sign a contract with the ball club that makes the best offer for my services."

The offers poured in. Granted they weren't for millions of dollars, but they were offers.

Bing Devine, the St. Louis Cardinals' general manager, offered one pennant, one bumper sticker, and a Cardinals jacket. "The jacket was a boys' large and was too small," said an unimpressed Hartwick.

Of the ten clubs that responded to his letter, most offers were similar to the one by Bill Veeck, then owner of the Chicago White Sox. Veeck wrote, "Because of your ingenuity, unusual approach and obvious sense of humor, we would be willing to waive the usual probation period for true blue, long-suffering, ever-loyal Sox fans to welcome you in our midst. If you find this a reasonable approach, we would be delighted to forward a multi-year fan contract for your signature."

"Big deal," Hartwick said. "You don't get a free agent fan for a scam like that."

So the search for a new team continued. Meanwhile, Hartwick was getting plenty of publicity. "It went from a funny little thing to a funny, sincere thing," he recalled. "I was outraged when *The Milwaukee Journal* said I was a publicity hound. Of course," he added, "it was true."

Finally Hartwick committed—to a minor league team.

But what an offer: The New Orleans Pelicans, the Cardinals' Triple A team, flew Hartwick and his wife to New Orleans and let him throw out the first pitch on Opening Day.

"In a way, I felt that I had sold myself out," Hartwick admitted. "I was like most every ballplayer. I went for the best offer."

His allegiance to the New Orleans Pelicans didn't last long, however. The team moved to Springfield, Illinois, the next year and somehow Springfield didn't have quite the allure that New Orleans did.

Hartwick remained in Grand Rapids and ultimately switched his support to the Cardinals. "I'm probably the only person in the world who gave up his allegiance to the Cubs and stuck with it," Hartwick said. ◇

Orioles' losing streak turns fan into a human sundae!

Diehard Baltimore Orioles fan Mike Filippelli wound up covered in gallons of chocolate syrup, whipped cream, and other toppings because his team let him down big time.

When the Orioles dropped their first ten games of the 1988 season, Filippelli, a disc jockey at WWTR-FM in Ocean City, Maryland, bet his broadcast partner Vince Edwards on the air that the losing streak would never reach 13 games.

It seemed like a safe bet since no major league team had ever gone more than 13 games before recording its first win at the start of a season.

But the O's lost more than 13 straight games—they dropped a record 21 in a row.

For Filippelli, a lifelong O's booster, losing the bet wasn't sweet. First, he crawled and walked 6.2 miles, which took four hours. Then he went to the Ocean Plaza Mall where, dressed in an Orioles jersey and a helmet, he sat down in a plastic kiddie pool. Next, Edwards dumped 30 gooey gallons of chocolate syrup over Filippelli's head.

Finally, mall patrons decorated Filippelli with cherries, pineapple, nuts, and whipped cream so he would be all decked out in his sundae best.

"After two hours of that, I can make it though a season of humiliation with the Orioles," said Filippelli. "It's something not to tell my grandchildren about." ◇

Twins Fans 'Back' Their Team

Minnesota fans lay on their backs in the street, shaking their arms and legs in a bizarre display of joy after the Twins won the 1987 World Series.

ERNEST HEMINGWAY: A quick kayo taught him to stick to his writing.

Hemingway Goads Pitcher Into a Boxing Match—And Gets Kayoed

Ernest Hemingway was a great writer who fancied himself as a macho man—but he picked on the wrong guy to show off his bravado.

In 1941, the Brooklyn Dodgers came to Havana, Cuba, for spring training. Hemingway, who lived in Havana and was a baseball fan, invited some players over to his house. After a few rounds of drinks, the writer boasted about what a good boxer he was. Then he pulled out two pairs of boxing gloves and declared that he would enjoy sparring with one of his guests.

Picking out what looked to him like an easy opponent, Hemingway challenged Dodgers relief pitcher Hugh Casey to a few rounds. The hurler declined, but Ernest insisted.

"Casey looked so innocent," recalled sports writer Red Barber, one of the guests that night. "He had a large stomach and rosy apple cheeks and spoke softly in his Georgia accent." What Hemingway didn't know was that Casey had been an amateur fighter—and a pretty good one—before he made it to the major leagues. Casey didn't want to box because he didn't want to hurt the famous author.

"But Hemingway wouldn't let me alone," Casey later told friends. "Finally I put on the gloves and he said we'd just fool around. Before I knew it, he was belting me as hard as he could. I told him to cut it out. He hit me harder than ever."

Hemingway wasn't the only tough guy around. The 6-foot, 2-inch, 210-pound Casey had his pride, too. And enough was enough.

Casey finally punched back at his host with a few solid combinations and then nailed him right in the jaw. "I knocked him down and out," said Casey. "That ended the boxing for the night." ◇

117

Poses as NFL-Star-Turned Ballplayer...

Imposter Dupes Tigers Into Ballyhooed Tryout

A fast-talking con man wrangled a much-publicized tryout with the Detroit Tigers after impersonating a fed-up pro football star who wanted to play baseball.

The classic hoax was pulled off in the spring of 1971 by 23-year-old William Douglas Street of Detroit who duped players, front office personnel, and reporters.

One day in early March, Street phoned Detroit farm director Hoot Evers and introduced himself as Jerry LeVias, star receiver of the Houston Oilers. "Levias" told Evers that he was tired of football and wanted to switch to baseball. He said he had played second base at Southern Methodist University and wanted a tryout with Detroit.

Evers said the Tigers would welcome him at spring training as long as he brought along written clearance from the Oilers. The fake LeVias then managed to get the phone number of Tigers star Gates Brown at his home in Detroit. The con man introduced himself as LeVias and said he was going to Lakeland, Florida, for a tryout. Then he asked Brown for a loan of $300 to finance the trip with a promise to pay him back once he signed a contract with the team. Amazingly, Brown agreed—and flew to Florida with him.

"Somebody in the front office gave him my phone number and that's why I thought he was okay," Brown said later.

When the bogus LeVias arrived at spring training without any baseball equipment or a letter from the Oilers, he claimed the airline had lost his luggage. The front office bought his lie.

The Tigers then issued a press release announcing that pro football star Jerry LeVias had agreed to terms and was at camp for a baseball tryout. Reporters and photographers watched his first workout and the reviews were mixed. Head scout Ed Katalinas told the press that LeVias had "unadulterated speed and great body control." But players and coaches thought he had a weak arm and an even weaker bat.

After the workout, "LeVias" held a press conference. "My two years with the Oilers were a mistake," he told reporters. "I'm tired of getting belted around. And the quarterbacks, they never throw to me because they're jealous of me."

He made great copy and the first story hit the Detroit streets the next day. That was the beginning of the end for "Jerry LeVias."

When wire services picked up the story, a Houston reporter promptly called the real Jerry LeVias at home to find out what was going on. "This is the biggest hoax I've ever heard of," said the stunned and angry football star.

That night Evers confronted the phony LeVias, who confessed that he had bamboozled the Tigers. "Actually my real name is Gerald Lee LeVias and I was an all-city football player at Central High in Detroit and spent two years in Vietnam. I just wanted a chance to show the Tigers that I could play baseball." He was lying about his past—but the Tigers believed him!

The team felt so sorry for him that it gave him a first-class plane ticket back to Detroit. He flew home without ever paying back Gates Brown. ◇

'GOOD OLD JOE EARLY NIGHT'

Indians Shower Fan With Gifts— Because He Asked Them to Do It!

Joe Early couldn't hit, field, or pitch. In fact, he never even played in a professional baseball game. But the Cleveland Indians honored him with his own "night" at the ball park simply because he asked them to do it.

In 1948, Early was a 26-year-old World War II veteran who worked as a night watchman at a local auto plant. He wrote a letter to the *Cleveland Press* complaining that teams were always holding "days" for well-paid stars who didn't need the money instead of for loyal fans who did. He suggested that he—as an average

follower of the Indians—deserved a night in his honor.

When Cleveland owner Bill Veeck, the king of baseball promotions, heard about the letter, he thought it was a great idea. He announced that the Indians would hold a "Good Old Joe Early Night" to honor the average

LIVELY GIFTS: Joe Early and his wife hold on tight to their presents.

119

fan—and that gifts would be given to him as well as the other spectators.

More than 60,000 fans turned out for the special night. Veeck spent $30,000 to fly in orchids from Hawaii which were given to the first 20,000 women in attendance that evening.

Before the game, Early and his wife were called out onto the field for the ceremony. The couple was then showered with presents—gag gifts at first. They were presented with an outhouse, a cow, a calf, a horse, and a backfiring Model T car. But just when

Early was beginning to think his special night was not such a good idea, Veeck presented him with some eye-popping gifts—including a new Ford convertible, a refrigerator, a washing machine, luggage, a watch, clothes, and a stereo system.

Fans in the stands weren't forgotten either. Through a drawing, hundreds of lucky fans won fancy prizes.

"Never in my wildest dreams did I think this would happen," said a gracious Early. "One thing is for certain. It never hurts to ask." ◇

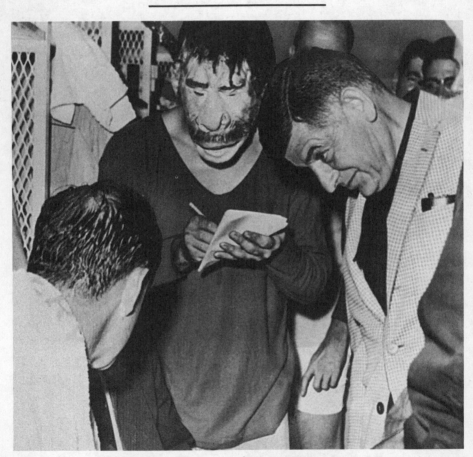

Happy Winners Mask Their Joy

Following the St. Louis Cardinals' pennant-winning game in 1964, catcher Tim McCarver clowns around wearing a Halloween monster mask while joining reporters in interviewing pitcher Barney Schultz.

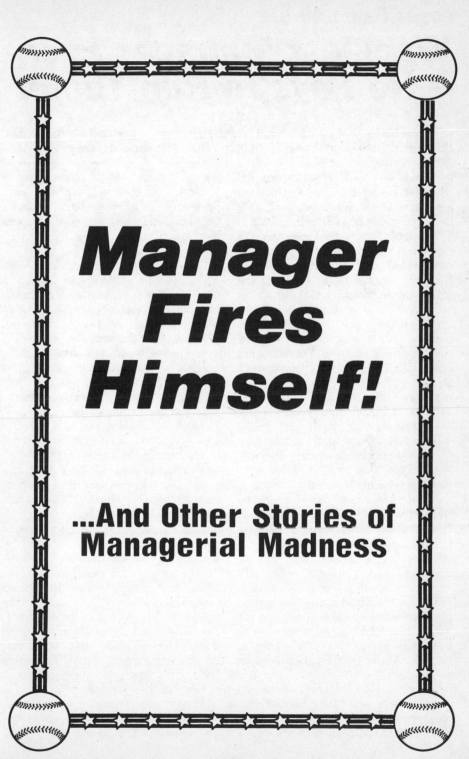

Manager Fires Himself!

...And Other Stories of Managerial Madness

Loses Game 40-5...

Wackiest Manager Ever —He Pays to Run Team!

In the history of professional baseball, no manager had more out-of-this-world bizarre coaching techniques than 75-year-old George Kromer.

His off-the-wall approach to the game was so astoundingly absurd that when he finally got a chance to manage his way, the team was annihilated 40-5.

In the spring of 1951 in the Class D Mississippi-Ohio Valley League, the club from Vincennes, Indiana, hired a new manager—75-year-old George Kromer. Well, actually, he hired the team. In an unusual twist—and an indication of the wacky things to come—Kromer *paid* the club to let him manage. He made the cash-starved team owners an offer they couldn't refuse. Kromer, who claimed he was a former ballplayer and minor league manager, gave them $5,000 with a promise of $5,000 more on June 1 if he could run the club.

The owners snapped up his offer. On the first day of spring training, Kromer sent everyone into a tailspin of disbelief with his far-fetched ideas.

"I was informed that this spring training would be different and would be run the right way," general manager Robert Rouse wrote in a letter to the league office. "The 'right way,' in part, consisted of using sponge rubber balls instead of baseballs, always throwing the ball in the infield to any base on two or more bounces, never using a glove or mitt to catch a ball, and to catch with both arms extended rigidly in front of you with all fingers spread apart as far as possible."

Kromer told players to avoid running or else they would tire themselves out. He ordered pitchers not to throw at any time other than in a game. "To warm up, a pitcher was to hold his arms upraised for 10 minutes," Rouse recalled. "He was then ready to go. To strengthen the eyes, players were asked to look into the sun for 15 minutes."

Obviously Rouse had to take drastic action. But he couldn't just dump the new manager—no matter how crazy his methods were—because Kromer had paid the owners to manage. Besides, they wanted the rest of his money—the $5,000 due June 1.

Rouse informed the players to pretend to listen to their manager but follow the orders from a veteran coach. The general manager also convinced Kromer he was too old to go on the road trips and to let the coach manage.

The team avoided disaster until that fateful day of June 17, 1951. With the coach ill and Rouse back in Vincennes, Kromer sneaked aboard the team bus and made a road trip to Danville, Illinois. Finally, Kromer had the chance to run the team exactly the way he wanted without interference.

"He submitted a lineup for the first game of a doubleheader that found outfielders pitching, pitchers in the infield, and infielders in the outfield," Rouse recalled. "The players tried to show Kromer that this was bad baseball but he replied that if they were ballplayers they could play just as well in one place as another."

The result was predictable: Vincennes "pitchers" gave up 32 hits and 13 walks. The fielders—only three of whom were in their normal positions—made eight errors. In a humiliating defeat, the team was crushed 40-5.

"After the unbelievable score, Kromer left the park and didn't return for three days," said Rouse. "When he did arrive, it was to brag about how he made headlines in papers all over the country as a result of the game at Danville."

Vincennes was not a bad team. In fact, after Kromer left, the club won the second game of the doubleheader 8-7.

Rouse tried one more time to talk some sense into Kromer, but the manager was determined to continue doing things his zany way. When he penciled in another lineup with players out of position, Rouse finally fired him—with the owners' blessing. Kromer had not come up with the $5,000 on June 1, so he was in default of his contract anyway. ◇

Heads Up Play

Oakland A's outfielder Billy North uses his glove for head protection to avoid getting pooped on by a flock of seagulls that invaded the Oakland Coliseum during a 1977 game with the Minnesota Twins.

Forgetful Manager Strolls Onto Field in His Underwear

As a minor league manager, Casey Stengel once became so wrapped up in his own pregame oratory, he forgot his pants—and walked out onto the field in his underwear!

The fans went crazy and the ramble-mouthed Stengel, for one of the rare times in his life, was left speechless.

In 1926, Casey was piloting the Toledo Mud Hens. Normally, he dressed in his uniform and then gave a pregame talk to the players. But on this particular day, he addressed the players while still in his underwear.

The speech was so powerful that even Stengel got caught up in it. Forgetting about his uniform, he followed his players from the clubhouse to the dugout and was intently studying his lineup card when he stepped onto the field. Suddenly, he heard laughter erupting from the stands.

The bewildered Casey looked around, wondering why all the fans were pointing and laughing. Then he glanced down and found the answer. He was still wearing his shorts and undershirt.

The Mud Hens later said they had never seen their manager run so fast as when Casey sprinted back into the clubhouse that day.

They also had never heard him so mum afterwards—because he refused to talk about his brief encounter with embarrassment. ◇

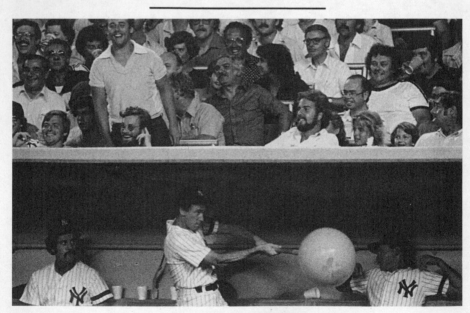

Balloon Ball

Sometimes the action at a baseball game isn't on the field. In this case, it's in the dugout where Yankee Fred Stanley swings at a large balloon that floated in from the stands during a 1980 game against the Orioles.

Manager's Grudge Keeps Pirates' Star Hitter Out of World Series

The Pittsburgh Pirates were humiliated in the 1927 World Series—because of the most incredible managerial snit ever. Pirates skipper Donnie Bush refused to play his star player, Kiki Cuyler, simply because Bush held a grudge against him.

In his first season at the helm of the Pirates, Bush astonished the baseball world by guiding the club to the pennant. That year, Cuyler batted .309—the fourth straight season he had hit over .300. The fleet-footed 26-year-old outfielder was the darling of Pittsburgh. He had been the hero of the 1925 World Series when he banged out seven hits and drove in six runs as the Pirates won only their second world championship ever.

The Pittsburgh faithful had high hopes that Cuyler would lead the club to another championship when the Pirates faced off against the New York Yankees in the 1927 fall classic.

But to the shocked outrage of the fans, Bush stubbornly and foolishly benched his star throughout the Series because the manager nursed a grudge against Cuyler that had been festering since midseason.

"During the season, Bush seemed to dislike me for no reason in the world," Cuyler recalled. Bush's animosity toward his star grew when Cuyler questioned the manager's decision to move him from third in the batting order to the second position.

The manager put the star in the doghouse for good after Cuyler failed to slide into second base in a game against the New York Giants.

"I was on first and the batter grounded to the second baseman," Cuyler recalled. "Instead of sliding into second, I went in standing up so that I could get hit by [shortstop] Travis Jackson's throw and prevent a double

KIKI CUYLER: Benched for Series.

play. But Jackson dropped the ball and tagged me out. Had I slid, I would have been safe. Because I failed to slide, Bush fined me $50 and benched me and refused to put me back in the lineup."

Pittsburgh fans were furious at Bush. They booed him every time he

125

stuck his head out of the dugout. At every home game, they chanted, "We want Cuyler! We want Cuyler!" and unfurled banners demanding Bush's ouster. Sportswriters wrote scathing articles condemning the manager's stubbornness. But Bush remained unmoved. "Nobody is going to tell me how to run my team," he declared.

During the Series, the hard-headed skipper refused to use Cuyler even as a pinch hitter. "I was left on the bench to watch the Pirates lose four straight games to the Yankees without getting a chance to stop the massacre," Cuyler lamented.

Cuyler never again played for the Pirates. He was traded to the Chicago Cubs where he played for seven years—batting over .317 in five of those seasons—and led the club to two pennants. In his 18-year career in the majors, Cuyler batted a remarkable .321, good enough to get him elected to the Baseball Hall of Fame.

But he never got to be a Series hero in 1927—because his manager held a grudge. ◇

Bosox Bubble Blower

Boston Red Sox pitcher Al Nipper turns into a real 'blowhard' after blowing up some bubblegum a foot in diameter while he sat in the dugout during a 1985 game with the Minnesota Twins.

Rangers Go Through Four Managers—In Six Days!

The Texas Rangers changed managers so often during one week that they should have installed a revolving door in their dugout.

In just six days, the club went through four managers: Frank Lucchesi, Eddie Stanky, Connie Ryan, and Billy Hunter.

The pilot parade began on June 22, 1977, when Lucchesi got the ax by the fourth-place Rangers who were sporting a mediocre 31-31 record.

Stanky, who last managed when he was guiding the Chicago White Sox nine years earlier, was brought in to replace Lucchesi. In his first game as the Rangers' skipper, the team beat the Minnesota Twins 10-8.

That night, Stanky returned to his hotel room, had a sleepless night, and realized he was a 60-year-old man whose family was more important than the Rangers. So after just 12 hours on the job, Stanky quit and flew back home to Mobile, Alabama, saying he missed his family.

On June 23, Rangers coach Connie Ryan was named acting manager. However, when he was offered the chance to finish out the year, he declined. So Texas owner Brad Corbett went hunting and hired Billy Hunter, third base coach for the Baltimore Orioles. The Rangers' fourth manager in six days lasted through the 1978 season and guided the team to two second-place finishes.

After Hunter's hiring, *The Sporting News* commented that "the Association of ex-Ranger Managers is one of the nation's fastest growing fraternities." ◇

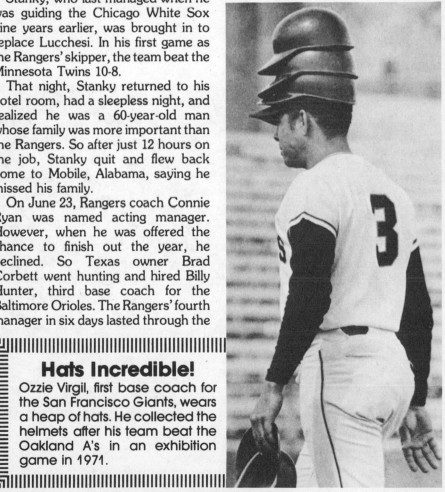

Hats Incredible!

Ozzie Virgil, first base coach for the San Francisco Giants, wears a heap of hats. He collected the helmets after his team beat the Oakland A's in an exhibition game in 1971.

Manager Steals Second Base —And Refuses to Give It Back

In the weirdest steal in baseball history, Tulsa Oilers manager Charlie Metro swiped second base —and he angrily refused to give it back!

It happened in 1966 in a minor league game between Tulsa and Denver. Oilers manager Charlie Metro, who had piloted the Chicago Cubs four years earlier, was furious with umpire Bruce Froemming, who later became a National League arbiter. The irate skipper blistered Froemming's ears with a stream of invectives over a call the ump had made at second. Finally, Froemming had heard enough and banished Metro from the game.

After delivering a few more choice words to the ump, Metro ripped second base from its mooring and then stomped off the field with the bag under his arm.

When the groundskeeper tried to retrieve the base from Metro, he angrily refused and disappeared into the clubhouse—still clutching the bag.

Play was held up for several minutes while the groundskeeper scrounged up another base. As for Metro, the league suspended him for three days and slapped him with a hefty fine for stealing second base. ◇

Mets 'Turf-Head'

A New York Mets fan wears a piece of sod over his head after watching his team clinch the division title in 1986. He and other jubilant fans had raced onto the diamond to tear up the turf for souvenirs.

Stengel to Stengel: "You're History!"

Manager Fires Himself

Casey Stengel was fired from his job as manager—by himself!

He was able to give himself the pink slip because he was also president of the club. However, he didn't fire himself because he thought he had done a lousy job. He did it because he had a better offer elsewhere.

It happened in 1925, early in Casey's managerial career. When the Ol' Professor was 35 years old, he was sent by the Boston Braves to their Worcester, Massachusetts farm club in the Eastern League as president, manager, and player. He played in 100 of 125 games as the club finished in third place.

"The job was all right," Casey explained later. "But I wasn't there very long before I received a better offer to manage Toledo, which was in a bigger league."

Casey asked the Braves to let him go—but was given a flat "no" by club boss Judge Emil Fuchs. So Stengel had to start his own "triple play." First, Casey the manager released Casey the player. Then came the second "out."

"As president of the Worcester Club, I had the right to hire and fire," recalled Stengel. "So I wired Judge Fuchs that President Stengel had just given Manager Stengel his unconditional release. That brought a hot rebuke back from Boston, which gave me an excuse to wire right back: 'This is to inform you that President Stengel resigns.'

"Then I wired Toledo that free-agent Stengel was prepared to sign up."

The ploy worked—and Casey became the only manager in baseball history to fire himself.

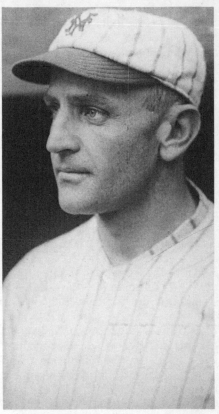

CASEY STENGEL fired himself because he had a better offer.

★★★

Hitter Has Exact Same Average 3 Years in Row!

Talk about amazing consistency! New York Mets outfielder Mookie Wilson hit for the exact same average three years in a row. Wilson, who was a regular starter, batted .276 in 1983, 1984, and 1985.

Rickey Manages Six Days a Week—But Never on Sunday!

Branch Rickey piloted the St. Louis Browns from 1913 to 1915 and the St. Louis Cardinals from 1919 to 1925—but never on Sunday.

In one of the weirdest managerial arrangements in major league history, Rickey would manage the team Monday through Saturday and then turn over the reins to player-coach Burt Shotton on Sunday.

When Rickey first took over as skipper of the Browns, he made it clear to management that the Sabbath was so important to him that he wouldn't even manage his team on Sunday if it were in the World Series. (He backed up his words much later when, as a club executive with the pennant-winning Brooklyn Dodgers, he didn't attend Series games on Sundays.)

With the Browns, Rickey had personal control of the club six days a week. But on Sundays, Rickey was never at the ball park. Although Shotton was not formally designated as interim manager, he was the one who made out the lineup card and called the shots during Sunday games.

He was so valuable to Rickey that when Rickey took over as skipper of the Cardinals, Shotton went with him as a player-coach-Sunday manager.

Unfortunately, it turned out to be a

BRANCH RICKEY: The Sabbath was very important to him.

case where two heads were not better than one. In ten years of the tandem managers, Rickey's teams finished fifth or worse eight times. The highest they ever finished was third. ◇

★★★

Spahn Throws Complete Game—Doesn't Get Win or Loss

In a pitching rarity, Warren Spahn of the Boston Braves tossed a complete game—yet he didn't get either a win or a loss.

In his rookie season in 1942, Spahn (0-0 at the time) started against the New York Giants. He was trailing 5-2 in the eighth inning when suddenly hundreds of young fans at the Polo Grounds poured out onto the field in a massive melee of mischief.

When order could not be restored, umpire Ziggy Sears forfeited the game to the Braves. Since forfeits are recorded as 9-0 victories without a winning or losing pitcher, Spahn got credit for a complete game—but was still sporting a record of 0-0.

Umpire Escapes Angry Mob — By Playing Dead!

...And Other Wild Stories About the Men in Blue

Medwick Called Out on Foul Ball That Lands in the Stands

Unbelievably, St. Louis Cardinals runner Joe "Ducky" Medwick was called out on a foul ball that was hit way back into the stands!

And it was all because of a dispute between two umpires.

In a 1935 game between the visiting Cardinals and the Cincinnati Reds, veteran arbiter Bill Klem, who was working the bases, was overruled by home plate umpire Ziggy Sears on whether a ball was hit fair or foul. Sears, only in his second year in the bigs, punctuated his decision by haughtily reminding the crusty Klem, "I'm the umpire-in-chief of this ball game."

Klem simmered at his upstart partner (there were only two umpires in those days) but said nothing to Sears until the sixth inning. With two out and Medwick running from first on the pitch, Pepper Martin fouled the ball back into the stands.

Medwick, who didn't realize the ball had been fouled, sprinted around second base and headed for third. Meanwhile, Reds catcher Gilly Campbell stuck his bare hand behind him and asked Sears for another ball. The ump handed him one.

"Campbell, just for the fun of it, whipped the ball down to our third baseman," recalled Reds manager Charlie Dressen. "The third baseman, also just for the fun of it, tagged Medwick coming into third.

"Then, of all things, home plate umpire Sears, rushing down to cover the play, called Medwick out—forgetting that the whole thing started on a foul ball. He even forgot he had handed a new ball to our catcher."

Naturally, the Cardinals went wild. Manager Frankie Frisch stormed out of the dugout and yelled, "Ziggy, have you gone crazy? How could the runner be out on a foul ball hit back into the stands?"

Amazingly, Sears stuck to his decision. Finally, in desperation, Frisch asked Sears to consult with Klem. Sears agreed and asked Klem, "Bill, what did you think of it?"

Now it was Klem's turn to get even with Sears. He stared Sears in the eye and snarled, "You said you were the umpire-in-chief around here, now start acting like one. I didn't see the play." Then Klem spun on his heels and returned to his position.

Recalled Dressen, "Klem saw the play all right, and knew it was a foul ball. But he let Sears stew. So the play stood, and we got Medwick out on a foul ball hit back into the stands." ◇

★★★

Like Father, Like Son

Boston Red Sox slugger Ted Williams, besides all his other feats and honors, holds the unique distinction of hitting a home run off both a father and his son.

During the 1940s, Williams clouted several homers off Chicago White Sox hurler Thornton Lee. Years later Thornton's son Don made it to the majors—and had about as much luck with the Splendid Splinter as Thornton did.

On Sept. 2, 1960, in the final month of his illustrious career, Williams faced Don, who was pitching for the Washington Senators. Like father, like son, Don gave up a round-tripper to Williams.

Convicted Murderer Granted Last Wish—Umpires Game!

In one of the most respectful games ever played, no one shouted, "Kill the umpire!" That's because everyone knew the umpire would be executed the very next day.

The game was played behind prison walls and was the last wish of umpire Patrick Casey—a convicted murderer.

At the turn of the century, Casey was an undistinguished minor leaguer who, when his playing days were over, became an umpire. Although he remained in the bushes, he loved his job and was a happy man. Unfortunately, life turned sour for Casey. First, he lost his umpiring job. Then came the tragedy in Nevada. In an uncontrollable rage, he murdered a woman and was sentenced to death.

In 1909, when the execution date was finally set and Casey knew he was going to die, he had one last request—to umpire a game one more time.

...and he's executed the very next day!

The warden at Nevada State Penitentiary rounded up two local teams who agreed to play on prison grounds so Casey could umpire his final game. He did such a fine job that no player questioned any of his decisions. When the game ended, players from both teams lined up, shook his hand, and congratulated him on his umpiring skills.

Patrick Casey walked off the field a contented man. The next day he was hanged. ◇

Ump, You're Out...of Uniform

Who's the guy on the right in the San Francisco Giants hat, jacket, and pants? It's umpire Ed Vargo! He and his fellow arbiters wore Giants uniforms during a 1983 game because their luggage got lost.

Illegal spitball invented by... an umpire!

The spitball—the illegal pitch that has baffled batters for decades—was not invented by a hurler but by a respected umpire!

The ump, George Hildebrand, was an outfielder playing for Providence, of the Eastern League, at the time. In 1902, Hildebrand was warming up before a game alongside pitcher Frank Corridon. Both were throwing to catcher Joe Brown.

As usual, the ballplayers were horsing around during the warmup. At one point, Corridon delicately moistened his finger tips and then, using a very exaggerated motion, threw a slow ball.

"Don't be so dainty," jeered Hildebrand. With that, he spat a generous gob on the ball and fired it to Brown. The ball broke sharply downward, astounding all three players.

"What did you do just then, George?" Brown asked.

"Show me what you did," an equally-impressed Corridon said. Hildebrand loaded up the ball again—and the spitball was born.

Corridon worked on the new pitch until he mastered it, and two years later he was in the major leagues. There, he threw the spitter for six years, compiling a career mark of 70-68 with a 2.80 ERA.

Hildebrand, who played in only 11 games for the Brooklyn Dodgers in 1902 before returning to the minors, passed the secret on to others. While in the Pacific Coast League, he met an old friend, Elmer Stricklett, a 27-year-old bush-league hurler whose arm was fading.

"How's everything, Elmer?" Hildebrand asked.

"Not so good," Strickland answered. "I've been getting my ears knocked off. I'm about through and should be getting my release any day now."

Hildebrand immediately showed him the spitter and Stricklett proceeded to become the hottest pitcher in the league, ripping off 11 straight victories. The next season he made it to the majors where he spent four years compiling an impressive lifetime ERA of 2.85.

Hildebrand, who traded in his uniform for the blue suit of an umpire, debuted as a major league arbiter in 1912. Eight years later, the spitball was outlawed. From then on, Hildebrand was put in the awkward position of policing the illegal pitch which he himself had invented. ◇

GEORGE HILDEBRAND: Father of the spitball.

Called a 'Blind Robber'...
Umpire Silences Heckling Giants With Rifle Shot!

Fed up with the barrage of insults hurled at him from members of the New York Giants, umpire Bob Emslie fired back—with a rifle.

Fortunately, he didn't aim at them. Instead, Emslie put on a brief shooting exhibition at the ball park to quiet his critics.

It all stemmed from a heated argument during a 1906 game in New York. Hot-tempered manager John McGraw called Emslie "a blind robber" and demanded he see an eye doctor. Several players joined McGraw in casting aspersions on the arbiter's eyes. Emslie was proud of his eyesight and wasn't about to take another potshot from anyone.

So the next morning, he showed up at the Giants' team practice—with a rifle under his arm.

Stunned players stared in fear of the ump. Visions of newspaper headlines like "Beserk Umpire Slaughters Players" blazed in their minds. They backed away, but Emslie didn't even glance at them.

Instead, he calmly walked out to second base, split a match, stuck a dime in the slit, and tucked the match in the ground. Then he strode back to home plate, lifted the rifle, and fired.

The dime went spinning into the outfield. The triumphant Emslie then walked proudly off the field. He never said a word.

The Giants never questioned Emslie's eyesight again. ◇

Hometown Boy

When pitcher Bill Voiselle was traded to the Boston Braves in 1947, he requested No. 96 because that's the name of his hometown—Ninety Six, South Carolina.

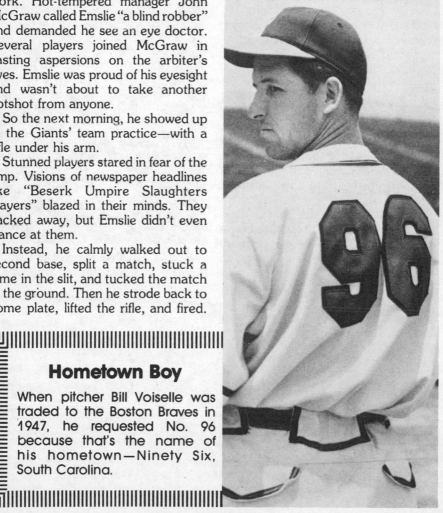

Exasperated Umpire Lets Beefing Batter Call Pitch!

Home plate umpire Jocko Conlan was so annoyed by batter Richie Ashburn's complaints of his ball and strike calls that the arbiter actually let Ashburn call a pitch.

Ashburn proved he was a better hitter than an umpire.

During a 1955 game, Conlan had just called a strike on the Philadelphia Phillies' star when Ashburn challenged the call. "No way, not close," he said to Conlan, along with a few other choice words about the umpire's eyesight.

"Okay," said Conlan. "*You* umpire. *You* call the next pitch."

Ashburn was so stunned that he took the next pitch. He looked back at Conlan and tentatively said, "Strike?"

"Strike!" Conlan shouted, throwing up his right arm after Ashburn called the pitch. Then the ump walked out in front of the plate and dusted it off. But before returning to his position, Conlan poked a finger in Ashburn's chest. "Richie," he said, "you just had the only chance a hitter has ever had in the history of baseball to bat and umpire at the same time—and you blew it!" ◇

JOCKO CONLAN gave a batter the chance to be an umpire.

Bonfire of the Insanities

Pepper Martin and Dizzy Dean, of the St. Louis Cardinals, really got "fired up" for a 1935 game.

Even though the blazing sun made the field so hot that players could've fried an egg on first base, the prank-loving pair built a bonfire in front of their dugout!

As sweating fans watched curiously, Martin and Dean began foraging for scraps of paper and pieces of wood. Then the firebrands piled the debris right outside the Cardinals' dugout and set the kindling ablaze.

Next, the zany duo got blankets, wrapped themselves up and sat Indian-style in front of the roaring flames—as fans gave their antics a warm reception with a roar of laughter.

Umpire Escapes an Angry Crowd—By Playing Dead!

International League umpire Tom Walker saved himself from an angry mob—by playing dead and having an ambulance drive him to safety.

In 1920, Walker was behind the plate in a crucial late-season game between the visiting Jersey City Skeeters and the Newark Bears. A Newark win meant a first place tie; a loss meant the Bears were out of the pennant chase.

Throughout the tense game, the hometown crowd howled at every call that went against Newark. The fans had worked themselves into a feverish state by the bottom of the ninth inning when the Bears, trailing 3-2 with two out, had the tying run on second base.

Then came the play of the day. The Newark batter cracked a single to center field and the runner on second tore around third and dashed toward the plate. The runner and the ball reached home plate at almost the same time.

As the cloud of dust settled, Walker boldly signalled the runner out—ending the game as well as Newark's pennant hopes.

But the call immediately triggered a storm of protest from the fans who swarmed onto the field and charged Walker. Surrounded by a squad of policemen, the brave ump managed to escape to the dugout amidst a hail of bottles and debris.

Once inside the clubhouse, Walker showered and dressed and prepared to leave. But the irate fans were still looking for blood. A huge mob had blocked the clubhouse doors, yelling for the umpire to come out. They shouted threats about "stringing the umpire up to a telephone pole."

Walker decided to wait out the crowd. So he sat inside. And waited. And waited. But the crowd refused to leave.

Finally, Walker decided to escape and devised a clever plan. First, he called the local hospital and summoned an ambulance to pick up a dying man in the clubhouse. Then the ump took off his coat, laid down on a rubbing table, and waited.

The ambulance pulled up to the clubhouse entrance and attendants rushed inside. Thinking he was dead, the attendants put Walker onto a stretcher and covered him with a sheet. They then wheeled the stretcher out through the unsuspecting crowd and into the ambulance, and drove off.

Once safely at the hospital, Tom Walker rose from the stretcher, donned his coat, bade the startled doctors and nurses goodbye, and headed for the railroad station. ◇

★★★

Down but Not Out

Veteran National League umpire Tom Gorman so loved his work that he took it to the grave with him. In 1986, Gorman was buried in his blue umpire's suit—with a ball and strike indicator in his hand. The count was 3 and 2.

Pirates-Dodgers Game Umpired By Two Players

A player from the Brooklyn Dodgers and one from the Pittsburgh Pirates were pressed into service as umpires for a doubleheader when both arbiters were seriously injured in freak accidents.

It happened on Aug. 20, 1912, during an era when only two umpires handled a major league game instead of the four that are now used.

In the bottom of the first inning of the opener at Forbes Field, umpire Bill Brennan was officiating the bases when Pirates runner Max Carey attempted a steal of second. Brennan ran toward the bag to call the play. But when he stopped too quickly on the grass near second, the arbiter slipped and fell over on his back.

Brennan, who lay motionless until several players came to his aid, had severely twisted his knee and torn several ligaments. He was carried off the field and taken to St. John's General Hospital in Pittsburgh.

Meanwhile, plate umpire Brick Owens announced that he would continue alone. Since Brennan had not made a call on Carey's attempted steal, Owens ordered the runner back to first base.

Owens had no trouble working the game solo—until he, too, was forced to leave by a serious injury.

In the bottom of the second inning, with the Pirates' Dot Miller at bat, a foul tip smacked Owens right below the chin, breaking his breastbone. The arbiter staggered and then collapsed. Owens then was rushed to the hospital where he joined his fellow umpire.

Now the teams were without any arbiter. Rather than call off the doubleheader, club officials agreed to use a player from each side to act as umpires. Dodgers utility catcher Eddie Phelps called balls and strikes while Pirates pinch hitter Ham Hyatt officiated the bases for the rest of the first game (won by Pittsburgh) and all of the second (won by Brooklyn). And they did it without any squawking from their fellow players.

"They did excellent work," reported *The Pittsburgh Post.* "The only sign of

...Fans cheer when umps are injured

displeasure was a dark look cast toward Phelps when he called a strike that greatly displeased [batter and teammate] Red Smith of the Dodgers."

In its account of the injuries to the two umpires, *The Brooklyn Daily Eagle* took exception to the Pittsburgh fans for laughing and cheering when the arbiters were injured.

"When Brennan's leg curled up under him and he went down in agony . . . the incident was hailed with blithesome uproariousness," said the *Eagle.* "And when Owens plunged forward on his face a few minutes later from a blow that may cause his death, it was greeted with a gale of glee.

"Why it should be excruciatingly comical to see a decent, upright, and hard-working citizen smashed so hard that he is almost paralyzed by pain is one of the mysteries of the American mind." ◇

★★★

Although 12 players in major league history have hit 50 or more homers in a single season, Hank Aaron—the all-time home run slugger—never hit more than 44 round-trippers in any one year.

138

Dodgers Executive Trades His Own Son!

...And Other Stories of Outlandish Deals

Hurler Finds His Poetry Pays; Deals Through Verse to Win a Raise!

Chicago White Sox relief pitcher Bobby Thigpen proved the pen was mightier than the agent when he used poetry to negotiate a new contract with his boss.

In his rookie season of 1987, Thigpen recorded 16 saves and sported a 7-5 mark while earning the major league minimum salary of $62,500.

When the White Sox offered him only a token raise to $70,000 for the 1988 season, Thigpen—who wanted his salary doubled—made this poetic appeal to White Sox Chairman of the Board Jerry Reinsdorf:

"As I sit home this off-season,
I wonder what the hell is the reason
Why the club wants to be unfair,
Underpaying a player who can produce and care."

Reinsdorf was unmoved by Thigpen's literary masterpiece—but the bullpen bard was undaunted. He was poetry in motion now, and he sent the owner another verse:

"Your name spelled backwards is Frodsnier,
And that rhymes with stingy cashier."

Thigpen fired off at least 10 poems at Reinsdorf before the chairman decided to retaliate with a literary effort of his own:

"I hope you are really a good pitcher,
Because as a poet you'll never get richer.
If you're not pitching this year,
I will be sad but won't fear;
Though you may be one of the best,
There's always someone among the rest."

Sticking up for his rights, Thigpen

BOBBY THIGPEN got poetic justice.

sent Reinsdorf a final poem:

"It's true my potential as a poet is very small,
But in the ninth, who do you want to have the ball?
You say there'll always be someone among the rest,
But who do you want, them or the best?"

Before the season started, Thigpen was happy to say . . . that the White Sox gave him a big increase in pay. ◇

Dodgers Executive Trades His Son!

When Al Campanis was put in charge of player personnel for the Los Angeles Dodgers in 1968, he showed there was no room for sentiment.

In his first official move following his promotion, Campanis peddled his own son! He sent his 24-year-old offspring, Jimmy, to the Kansas City Royals for a couple of minor leaguers.

It was Al who first signed Jimmy, a catcher, to a contract with the Dodgers' organization six years earlier. Jimmy spent most of those years in the minors although he had a few brief stints with the Dodgers as their third-string catcher.

Just two weeks before Christmas in 1968, the club's newly-appointed vice president phoned his son and said, "Jimmy, this is Dad. I just swapped you to Kansas City for two minor leaguers to be named later."

(It turned out not to be a big deal. Jimmy played only 67 games over three seasons and ended his career with a woeful .147 batting average.)

The first person to phone Al after the

AL CAMPANIS proved that he didn't play favorites—by trading his son.

transaction was Bess Campanis, Al's wife and Jimmy's mother. "Now I can tell you, Al," she said. "I've been an American League fan for some time now." ◇

★★★

TTTriple TTTrouble!

Lead-off triples spelled doom for the Louisville Colonels in a 1928 game against the Kansas City Blues.

In the top of the ninth inning of a 3-3 tie, Louisville's Joe Guyon belted the first pitch from Heinie Meine for a triple. Meine then walked the next two batters, loading the bases with no out. However, the hurler frustrated the Colonels by getting the next three outs without letting a run score.

Incredibly, in the top of the 11th inning, Guyon once again led off with a triple. And once again, Meine walked the next two batters before disposing of the following three without any damage—much to the growing dismay of the Colonels.

In the 13th inning, the unbelievable happened—Guyon smacked his third consecutive lead-off triple. And for the third time, the Colonels loaded the bases with no one out. And for the third time, Meine wiggled out of the jam.

By now, the Colonels were suffering severe mental trauma. So Meine put them out of their misery. He led off the bottom of the 13th frame with a game-ending, game-winning home run!

Catcher Swapped for Announcer

A baseball player was traded for a radio announcer.

It happened in 1948 when famed sportscaster Red Barber, the voice of the Brooklyn Dodgers, became seriously ill and the Dodgers needed a temporary substitute.

Dodger executive Branch Rickey heard about Ernie Harwell, who was then a young announcer under contract to the minor league Atlanta Crackers. Rickey called Atlanta club owner Earl Mann and asked if he could hire Harwell. But Mann balked at letting the announcer out of his contract—unless the Crackers received "compensation."

"We need a catcher," Mann told Rickey. So Rickey sent catcher Cliff Draper from the Dodgers' farm team in Montreal to Atlanta. And the Crackers sent Harwell to the Dodgers.

Draper never made it to the majors. But Harwell lasted more than 40 years in the bigs as an announcer, 31 of them with the Detroit Tigers. ◇

Bees Swarm Reds Dugout

Two fans carefully remove a bee-covered microphone from the roof of the Cincinnati Reds dugout before a 1976 game with the San Francisco Giants which was delayed 45 minutes by the buzzing swarm.

Players Swapped During Twin Bill Finish Day With Opposing Teams

Max Flack started the day playing for the Chicago Cubs and finished it playing for the St. Louis Cardinals.

Meanwhile, Cliff Heathcote started the same day playing for the Cardinals—and ended it playing for the Cubs.

In one of the strangest trades in baseball, the two outfielders were swapped for each other between games of a doubleheader.

On May 30, 1922, the Cardinals and Cubs squared off in a morning-afternoon doubleheader. In the opener, Flack started for the Cubs in right field and went 0-for-4 while Heathcote, playing center field for the Cardinals, went 0-for-3.

During the break, the Cubs sent Flack, 32—who was batting only .222

following back-to-back .300-plus seasons—to the Cards for Heathcote, 24, who was hitting .245. The two players then donned their new uniforms and played against their former teammates in the nightcap.

The change apparently did some good. Flack went 1-for-4 and Heathcote 2-for-4. Flack played three more years with the Cardinals before retiring while Heathcote stayed with the Cubs for eight more seasons. ◇

★★★

Hurler Burned From Ironing Shirt — While He's Still Wearing It!

Atlanta Braves pitcher John Smoltz was both red-faced and red-chested after he burned himself from ironing a shirt—while he was still wearing it!

During spring training in 1990, Smoltz was in his hotel room when he decided to get the wrinkles out of his Polo shirt. But no one was there to suggest that he first take off the shirt. The result was five inch-long red streaks burned into the right side of his chest.

Incredibly, that wasn't the first time Smoltz ironed his shirt that way. "I've ironed my shirt while wearing it five or six times before and never was burned," Smoltz said. "I couldn't believe it."

Indians Fairy Loses To Red Sox Witch

After a self-proclaimed witch said she helped the Boston Red Sox beat the Cleveland Indians in a 1976 game, the Tribe responded by hiring a fairy godmother. Despite her magic wand, the Indians lost again 7-5.

Zaniest Trades

Players—including some well-known stars—have been swapped for some of the strangest things. For example:

- Before he made it to the bigs and became a Hall of Fame pitcher, Lefty Grove was traded by the Martinsburg, West Virginia, club to Baltimore of the International League in 1920—for a new outfield fence!
- Joe Engel, owner of the Chattanooga Lookouts swapped shortstop Johnny Johns for a live turkey in 1930.
- Joe Martina, Texas League pitching star, was traded in 1921 from Dallas to New Orleans for two barrels of oysters. He was known thereafter as "Oyster Joe."

- Cy Young was once shipped from Canton to Cleveland, in 1890, for $250 and a suit of clothes.
- First baseman Jack Fenton was traded by a minor league San Francisco team for a box of prunes.
- When the St. Louis Browns ended spring training in Montgomery, Alabama in 1913, they left infielder Buzzy Wares behind—as payment for the use of the Montgomery team's ball park.
- In 1989, pitcher Tom Fortugno of the Reno club was sold to Stockton for $2,500 and 144 baseballs.
- Mike Dondero, infielder for San Antonio, was almost traded for a dozen doughnuts in 1928. As a joke, Dallas owner Louis Schepps—who also owned a bakery—offered the sweet deal to San Antonio owner Homer Hammonds, who agreed. Schepps then phoned his bakery and had a dozen crullers delivered to his office. Recalled Hammonds, "I called the deal off when Schepps ate five of the doughnuts." ◇

This Leadoff Batter Is 100 Years Old!

After celebrating his 100th birthday in 1985, Freddy Broadwell of St. Petersburg, Florida, continued to play softball with the world-renowned Kids & Kubs. Only men over the age of 75 can join the teams which have been in existence since 1940. The elderly players—clad in black bowties, white shirts, and white pants—play three times a week.

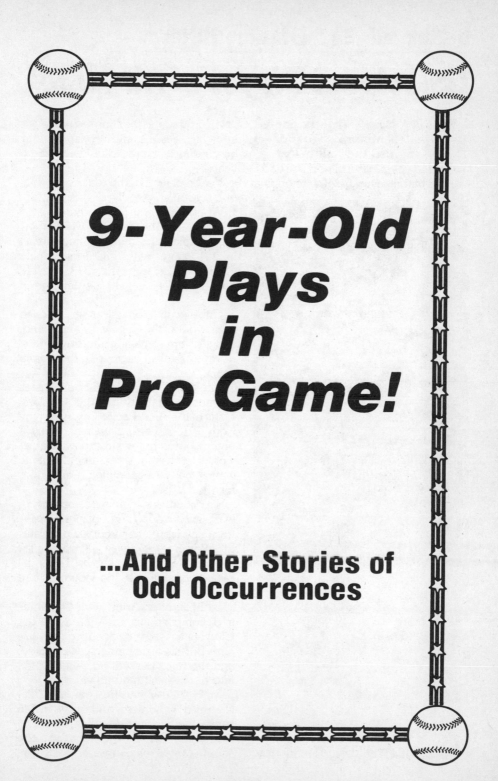

9-Year-Old Plays in Pro Game!

...And Other Stories of Odd Occurrences

III-Starred .341 Lifetime Hitter...

Unluckiest Player of All Time!

Russell "Buzz" Arlett—named The Greatest Minor Leaguer of All Time—was also the unluckiest.

After 17 years in the minors, he had a lifetime batting average of a whopping

"BUZZ" ARLETT: A very unlucky guy.

.341, drove in 100 or more runs eight straight seasons, and bashed four homers in a game twice in the same year.

Yet he played in the majors for only one season!

What's all so curious is that Arlett's one year in the majors was just as remarkable as his minor league career. In 121 games with the Philadelphia Phillies in 1931, he hit .313 with 18 homers and a slugging percentage of .538.

Unbelievably, Buzz was sent back to the minors the following year and, despite his amazing batting feats, never was called back up to the majors again.

The 6-foot, 3-inch, 225-pound mass of muscle starred for the Oakland Oaks of the AAA Pacific Coast League from 1918-30. Arlett was not only a potent hitter but a superb pitcher as well. He was a three-time 20-game winner before becoming an outfielder for the Oaks.

Teammates, managers, coaches, and even opposing players were mystified why, after being such a star for 12 years, Buzz was still waiting for the call to the big show. The only conclusion: he was the victim of bad luck.

In 1923, after Arlett won 25 games and compiled an ERA of 2.77, the Cincinnati Reds decided to acquire him. But his arm suddenly went lame, and the Reds passed. So Buzz turned into a power-hitting outfielder.

In 1924—when he batted .328, slammed 33 homers, and drove in 145 runs—the St. Louis Cardinals were all set to buy Buzz. But first, their top scout wanted one more look. It was just Arlett's luck that on the day the scout watched him, Buzz, considered a decent fielder, was hit on the head by a fly ball. The scout decided to pass.

Over the next couple of years, other teams expressed an interest in Arlett, but backed off because the Oakland management wanted too much money for him.

Then in 1930, it looked like Buzz was going to get his first big break. The Brooklyn Dodgers sent a scout to arrange for Arlett's long-awaited promotion to the majors.

But on the very day the deal was to be made, Arlett got into an argument with an umpire. The arbiter whacked Buzz on the head with his mask so hard that the hard-luck player was knocked out of action for three weeks. Because the Dodgers needed a new outfielder immediately, they brought up his teammate, Ike Boone, instead.

Arlett was 32 years old before he finally got his chance with the Phillies in 1931. He played just as superbly as he had in the minors. But for some mysterious reason, Buzz was sent down to the International League the following season. He played five more years in the minors and was still hitting over .300 when he finally retired.

How could a player perform so well for so long in the minors and then demonstrate that he could hit major league pitching and play only one year in the bigs?

"Baseball 'experts' are a hardheaded bunch," one historian noted acidly. "A lot of times they think they know better than any statistical line and no amount of facts will change them. If they don't like a player in the minors for some obscure reason, they aren't about to change their opinion—for any reason."

Years after Buzz died in 1965, the Society of American Baseball Researchers named him The Greatest Minor Leaguer of All Time. They could have added The Unluckiest. ◇

Major Leaguer Ejected From Game Without Ever Having Played in One!

Basketball Hall of Famer Bill Sharman left his mark on the baseball diamond as well as the court.

Before becoming an NBA legend for the Boston Celtics, Sharman was a minor league outfielder who was called up by the Brooklyn Dodgers toward the end of the 1951 season.

On September 27, the Dodgers and Boston Braves were locked in a 3-3 tie when plate umpire Frank Dascoli called Braves runner Bob Addis safe at home on a close play.

The Dodgers' bench exploded in rage and heaped verbal abuse on the ump. In retaliation, Dascoli ordered a mass ejection, clearing the entire Brooklyn dugout. That included the rookie Sharman, who was sitting at the end of the bench.

Sharman never did play in the majors and finished his baseball career a year later down in the minors. He then went on to basketball fame with the Celtics . . . but not before leaving a baseball legacy of his own as the only major leaguer ever thrown out of a game without ever having played in one. ◇

★★★

In 1950, Philadelphia Athletics manager Connie Mack and Brooklyn Dodgers manager Burt Shotton were not allowed to go onto the field—even to change pitchers. That's because they managed in street clothes and major league rules stated only those in uniform could be on the field.

147

Over 50, but Not Over the Hill...

Baseball's Amazing Graybeards

Although baseball may be a young man's game, major leaguers over the age of 50 have stolen bases, tossed shutout innings, and banged out base hits.

On Sept. 25, 1965, Satchel Paige became the oldest player ever to appear in a major league game when he pitched three scoreless innings for the Kansas City Athletics against the Boston Red Sox. The aging hurler was 59 years old when he was reactivated as a promotional stunt after 12 years of retirement. He walked one, struck out one, and gave up only one hit, to Carl Yastrzemski, who had the league's best slugging percentage that year.

Prior to Paige, the oldest major league player was the Washington Senators' Nick Altrock, who pinch-hit in a game in 1933 when he was 57. He grounded out.

That was fortunate for Minnie Minoso, of the Chicago White Sox. In 1976, at the age of 53, Minoso set the record for being the oldest player to get a hit in a major league game when he singled. Minoso has the distinction of playing in five decades in the bigs. He started in 1949 and retired in 1964. However, the White Sox reactivated him for three games in 1976 and two games in 1980.

Although 50-year-old Arlie Latham had slowed down somewhat because of age, the player-coach for the New York Giants still had enough spring in his legs to become the oldest player ever to steal a base.

The two oldest regular roster players of all time were both pitchers: knuckleballer Hoyt Wilhelm and spitballer Jack Quinn. Wilhelm was five days short of his 49th birthday when the Dodgers—his eighth team in

SATCHEL PAIGE was the oldest player in a big league game.

21 years—released him in 1973.

Quinn, who played on nine clubs in 23 years, was 50 years old when he was released. Quinn is the oldest pitcher ever to win a game—at age 49. He's also the oldest hurler ever to lose one, too—at age 49. ◇

Baseball-Hating Fiancee Forces Superstar to Quit!

Bill Lange—the greatest and most popular outfielder of his time—was forced to quit the game at the height of his career because his fiancee was a society girl who hated baseball.

Lange was the game's first true superstar. Throughout the 1890s, the handsome 200-pound, 6-foot, 2-inch slugger played center field for the Chicago White Stockings (forerunners of the Chicago Cubs). From 1892-99, he averaged 64 stolen bases a season, batted better than .300 for six straight years and was known as a sensational, flashy outfielder.

Lange, who had an ever-present and contagious smile, enjoyed an immense personal following of thousands of fans who went to the game solely to see him, rather than the team, play. *The Chicago Tribune* said at the time that Lange was "the greatest masher who ever trod State Street or Broadway." Whenever Lange arrived in a city on the National League circuit, dozens of scented notes addressed to him from swooning female fans were piled up on the desk at the hotel. Lange did his best not to slight any one of them.

Despite the shower of adulation, Lange's days as a bachelor and ballplayer were numbered. At the turn of the century—when he had reached the height of his career as a big league superstar—Lange fell head over heels in love. His heart had been captured by Grace Geiselman, a young lady of high social standing in San Francisco.

Just months before the start of the 1900 season, Lange proposed to the society girl. Grace let him have her hand in marriage—on one condition. He had to quit baseball. Grace found the game simply too undignified. To her, baseball was played in filthy parks by foul-mouthed, tobacco-spitting men in knee breeches. It mattered not that her fiance was the game's greatest, most popular outfielder of his day.

Although Lange was only 28 years old and at the peak of his career, he was a man easily swayed by the power of love. To please the whim of the woman of his dreams, he agreed to give up baseball.

Fans, teammates, and opposing players were shocked when word reached them that Lange had hung up his spikes for good. The White Stockings offered to double his salary if he'd return. But he refused.

With deeply felt mixed emotions, he wrote a farewell note to his teammates. It read: "Plant flowers on my baseball grave in center field, for I will never play there again. For I am a man in love!"

Lange never did play again—all because of his undying love for a woman who hated baseball. ◇

★★★

Now *That's* a Hitter!

In an odds-defying feat, the Detroit Tigers' Tony Phillips rapped singles that struck base runners—in back-to-back games! On Sept. 27, 1991, Phillips smacked a hot shot grounder that nailed his teammate, Milt Cuyler, who was running from first. Cuyler was automatically out.

The next day, with Skeeter Barnes on base, Phillips blasted a liner that grazed the runner for another hit—and another out. "I don't remember hitting anybody like that before," said Phillips. "So it was strange to see it happen two days in a row."

149

Player Pinch-Hits and Pinch-Runs In Same Game

Pat Collins, of the St. Louis Browns, holds the unique distinction of being the only player ever to pitch-hit and pinch-run in the same game.

It happened on June 8, 1923, during an era when the rules on pinch runners were much more relaxed. In a game against the Philadelphia Athletics, Browns third baseman Homer Ezzell was a runner on first in the third inning when he needed to go to the bathroom and called timeout. The Browns asked A's manager Connie Mack if they could have a courtesy runner for Ezzell while he heeded the call of nature. No problem, said Mack.

So Collins went in as a pinch runner. Collins didn't score and when the inning was over, Ezzell returned to the game while Collins returned to the bench.

In the ninth inning, Collins was sent in to pinch-hit for pitcher Ray Kolp—even though, according to the rules, he had made an earlier appearance and had left the game. Collins walked. Ironically, he was then replaced with another pinch runner. Collins headed back to the dugout as the only player to pinch-hit and pinch-run in the same game. ◇

'Martians' Invade Comiskey Park!

The Martians are coming! The Martians are coming! In a scene out of a grade B science fiction flick, the Chicago White Sox were invaded by space aliens wielding ray guns. Actually this was just another of owner Bill Veeck's crazy promotional stunts. He hired four midgets to dress up as little men from Mars and "attack" the White Sox dugout before a game played at Comiskey Park on May 26, 1959.

52-Year-Old Catches Giants' Flag-Clincher!

Although he was 52 years old and hadn't played in the major leagues for nearly 11 years, Jim O'Rourke returned to the bigs solely to catch the game in which the New York Giants clinched the 1904 National League pennant.

O'Rourke—who had an 18-year career in the majors, including seven seasons with the Giants—was living in Bridgeport, Connecticut, managing a minor league team when he came up with a great idea. The Giants were only one game away from winning the pennant and O'Rourke wanted to be a part of the historic moment. So he hopped a train to New York and begged Giants manager John McGraw to let him catch for just one inning in the next game.

"You're 52 years old," McGraw growled. "It's out of the question."

O'Rourke continued to plead, pointing out that he had kept himself in shape by catching for the minor league team in Bridgeport. Besides, the Giants had a huge 10-game lead over the second-place Chicago Cubs. McGraw still said no.

But O'Rourke wouldn't give up. He tracked down the Giants' star pitcher, "Iron Man" Joe McGinnity, and begged him to intercede. Touched by the aging catcher's plea, McGinnity, who was scheduled to start the next game, convinced McGraw to start O'Rourke.

The next day O'Rourke proudly strode onto the field at New York's Polo Grounds in a Giants uniform. He played so well in the first inning that McGraw decided to leave him in for the next two frames.

In the third inning, O'Rourke came to bat—and swatted a single. When the left fielder bobbled the ball, O'Rourke raced to second and then on to third after a wild throw.

Moments later, O'Rourke scored on a hit. McGraw was so impressed that he left the old man in for the entire game.

O'Rourke went 1-for-4 as the Giants won the game—and clinched the pennant.

The next day, O'Rourke went back home a happy man. He set a record—one that still stands—for being the oldest major leaguer ever to play a full game.

And he proved that though long of tooth, he still had what it took to compete in the bigs. ◇

★★★

Browns Use 9 Pitchers —One Per Inning!

On the final day of the 1949 season, the seventh-place St. Louis Browns used a hurler per inning in a game against the sixth-place Chicago White Sox.

As a stunt to finish out the dismal year, the Browns decided to let every pitcher on their staff toss one inning. Starting pitcher Dick Starr threw in the first frame followed by Ned Garver, Joe Ostrowski, Cliff Fannin, Tom Ferrick, Karl Drews, Bill Kennedy, Al Papai, and Red Embree.

Despite a fresh arm each inning, the Browns still lost 4-3. Kennedy took the loss.

Baseball's Youngest Player...

9-Year-Old Plays in Pro Game!

The youngest person ever to play professional baseball was only nine years old!

Grade schooler Willie Diggins was paid $5 to play right field for Manchester for one inning in a 1905 game against Lowell in the New England League.

During the contest, Manchester player-manager Win Clark and two others were kicked out of the game by the umpire. The club now had just enough men to field a team. Clark was hoping no one else would get ejected or hurt because there was no one left on the bench. However, Willie's dad, catcher Bill Diggins, was suffering from a severe hangover and "was pretty shaky," Clark recalled.

Manchester managed to hold onto a three-run lead until the eighth inning when Lowell loaded the bases on three walks. "With the count three-and-two on the next batter, our pitcher fired a strike, but the ball bounced off Diggin's glove and rolled underneath a bench," recalled Clark. "Bill reached down for it, fell flat on his face, and all four runs scored."

Clark, still managing even though technically he had been thrown out of the game, was so furious at Diggins that he yanked him from the contest. But that left the team with only eight players. Clark ordered the right fielder to play catcher. Then, in desperation,

Clark turned to Diggins' son, Willie, who was quietly sitting on the bench, and offered him $5 to play right field. The youngster jumped at the chance, grabbed a glove, and raced out to his position.

But no balls were hit to him. It seemed that his appearance in the game would not affect the outcome one way or the other.

But in the ninth inning, Manchester loaded the bases with two out and one run down when Willie came to bat. "I told him that if he'd just stand there, the pitcher would walk him because he was so small," Clark said.

The first two pitches were balls. Then the Lowell hurler threw a really slow pitch that Willie couldn't resist swinging at. He missed. Clark rushed out to the batter's box and reminded the boy to keep the bat on his shoulder. Willie then took a ball and a strike to run the count full.

"I swear the next pitch was two feet over Willie's head—but the umpire called it a strike, ending the game," recalled Clark.

The manager went berserk. He grabbed a bat and struck the ump on the chest protector, knocking him down and triggering a near riot. Order was finally restored.

As for young Willie Diggins, he never again played for a professional team.

Bud Clancy of the Chicago White Sox and Jimmy Collins of the Chicago Cubs had the laziest days ever for first basemen on Sept. 27, 1930 and June 29, 1937, respectively. They each played a full nine-inning game without touching the ball. No putouts, no assists, no errors.

Player Changes Name—To Make Sure He'd Get Paid!

John Jacob Zimmerman changed his name to Jake Atz—so he could get paid.

In 1900, Zimmerman, a 21-year-old infielder, played on a minor league team that, like so many other struggling clubs, had a frequent cash flow problem. His team sometimes had trouble meeting its payroll. The players were required to line up at the pay window in alphabetical order. But on more than one occasion, the money ran out before the last man got to the window—and that last man was always Zimmerman.

When Zimmerman was traded to another club, he debated whether or not to continue his baseball career because of the uncertainty of getting paid. He decided to stick it out only after he came up with a plan to avoid getting shut out financially.

Although he was proud of the name he was born with, Zimmerman changed his name to Jake Atz. That way he was sure to be at or near the front of the pay line. It worked. He never had to worry about receiving a paycheck again.

Atz eventually reached the majors as an infielder for the Chicago White Sox. But even though he was in the bigs and was assured of getting paid, he never changed his name back. ◇

Catch Her — If You Can!

Minnesota Twins right fielder Hosken Powell tosses a life-sized inflatable doll into the stands. It was thrown onto the field at Comiskey Park during a 1980 game with the Chicago White Sox.

Composer of Baseball's Theme Song Had Never Seen a Game

Baseball's immortal theme song, "Take Me Out to the Ball Game," was composed by a man who had never even seen a baseball game.

Singer-songwriter Jack Norworth just didn't have any interest in the national pastime. But Norworth, whose sole passion was entertaining people, recognized the importance of baseball to other Americans. So he sat down one morning in 1908 and batted out the words and music to "Take Me Out to the Ball Game." He then introduced it in his stage act that very same night.

While he was singing it, Norworth became a little worried about the audience reaction, since he had never seen a game. But he needn't have been concerned—the audience went crazy and demanded that he sing it over and over again. Before long, the tune swept the country and became the grand old game's theme song.

Norworth appreciated the acclaim—and the money—that he received from the song. But he never

JACK NORWORTH wrote "Take Me Out to the Ball Game."

did take an interest in baseball. In fact, the composer of "Take Me Out to the Ball Game" never did see his first ball game until 34 years after he wrote the song! ◇

Indoor Game Is Rained Out!

The June 15, 1976 game between the visiting Pittsburgh Pirates and the Houston Astros was rained out—even though the game was to be played indoors in the Astrodome.

When ten inches of rain fell on Houston that day, the areas around the stadium were under water, some as much as five feet deep. While the players had arrived early before the flooding grew worse, most fans and ball park personnel couldn't get anywhere near the Astrodome.

By game time, only 30 hardy fans had managed to trek through the flooded streets and make it to the stadium. But no one else did—not even the four-man umpiring crew.

After calling the game because of the floods, club officials invited the fans and players from both teams to dine on steak and fried chicken at a buffet set up in the infield. There, they toasted baseball's first "rain-in."

154

Sportswriter Helps Win Game For Pirates!

A Pittsburgh sportswriter helped the Pirates snatch victory from the jaws of defeat.

During a 1948 game, the Pirates and visiting Dodgers engaged in a wild slugfest. Trailing 11-9 in the bottom of the ninth inning, Pittsburgh launched a last-ditch rally and put runners on first and second with two outs. So Dodgers manager Burt Shotton replaced pitcher Hugh Casey with Carl Erskine. Facing batter Eddie Bockman, Erskine threw three balls and a strike. A nervous Shotton then replaced Erskine with bullpen ace Hank Behrman. Behrman immediately retired Bockman to win the game for the Dodgers.

Or so everyone thought. Except Pittsburgh sportswriter Les Biederman. Up in the press box, the scribe realized that the Dodgers had violated a rule that even the umpires had overlooked. A relief pitcher has to pitch to at least one batter before he could be replaced. Erskine had left the game with the count 3-and-1 without having finished pitching to Bockman, the only batter he had faced.

Biederman quickly relayed the information to Pirates manager Billy Meyer, who protested the game.

To Pittsburgh's joy, the protest was upheld. National League President Ford Frick ordered the game resumed at the point where Erskine was given the hook.

So two weeks before the end of the season, the two teams picked up where they left off in the bottom of the ninth inning with Pirates on first and second and two outs. Returning to the mound with a 3-and-1 count on Bockman, Erskine walked him on the next pitch to load the bases. Manager Burt Shotton immediately called on Hank Behrman to pitch to the next batter, Stan Rojek.

After running the count to 3-and-2, Behrman went into a full windup. With all three runnners taking off on the pitch, Rojek ripped a fastball off the glove of third baseman Tommy Brown. The ball bounded into left center for a dramatic, bases-clearing, game-winning double.

Although Rojek delivered the key blow in the Pirates' stunning 12-11 win, the real hero of the game was a sharp sportswriter who knew the rules even better than the umpires. ◇

★ ★ ★

Hall of Famer Used the Same Bat for 14 Years!

Hall of Fame shortstop Joe Sewell used the same bat in every one of his 14 years in the majors without breaking it.

"I called the bat Black Betsy," said Sewell, who played for the Cleveland Indians and New York Yankees from 1920-34. In the first two months of each season, he used the 40-ounce bat and then switched to a 36-ounce bat. "I got more than 1,000 hits from Black Betsy," added Sewell, who swatted 2,226 hits in his career.

He still had the remarkable bat when he was inducted into the Baseball Hall of Fame. How did he keep it from breaking during his playing days? Maybe it was the strange way he kept the bat in shape—he rubbed it with chewing tobacco and rolled it with a Coca-Cola bottle!

Detroit Infielder Jailed—For Pulling Hidden-Ball Trick!

Detroit Tigers second baseman Germany Schaefer was arrested and locked up in jail—for doing nothing more than executing to perfection the hidden-ball trick.

Schaefer was obsessed with pulling the trick on unwary runners at second base and became very adept at it. He even tried the scam during the 1907 World Series with the Chicago Cubs, but without success. Undaunted, he attempted it later that winter when the Tigers went to Cuba on a barnstorming trip to play Havana's best teams.

In one of the games, the score was tied in the bottom of the ninth with the winning run on second for the Cuban team when Detroit pitcher George Mullin called time and summoned Schaefer to the mound.

"See if you can get that guy on second," Mullin whispered as he secretly slipped the ball to Schaefer. The second sacker slyly hid the ball in his glove and trotted back to his position.

As Mullin stepped back on the mound, the runner edged off second base, and Schaefer slapped on the tag.

"You're out!" yelled the American ump. The Cuban fans were outraged and stormed onto the field, wanting to tear the flesh off Schaefer and the umpire. Police rushed out and managed to protect the player and ump from the wild crowd.

After a few tense minutes, the cops restored order. But then they grabbed Schaefer, announced he was under arrest, and hauled him off to jail. Despite his pleas of innocence, the shocked player spent the night in a dirty cell.

The next morning, Germany was brought before a judge who snorted that the player's hidden-ball ploy was a "shabby trick." The judge then leaned over the bench and growled, "I ought to keep you in jail for a week." But after a stern lecture about fair play, the judge told the shaken Schaefer he was free to go.

Not until Germany returned home after the barnstorming trip did he learn that he had been framed—by one of his own teammates! Mullin, a notorious prankster, had set the whole thing up. Shortly after the team had arrived in Cuba, the hurler had bribed the police to "arrest" Schaefer the first time he pulled the hidden-ball trick.

Everything went according to plan—except for the riot. It's not known how Germany got his revenge. ◇

★★★

The Most Even Pennant Races in History

In an odds-defying season, the New York Yankees and Brooklyn Dodgers experienced identical pennant races in 1949.

Each club won 97 and lost 57. Each team finished one game ahead of the second-place club. The Yankees beat out the 96-58 Boston Red Sox and the Dodgers did likewise to the 96-58 St. Louis Cardinals.

But the similarities ended when it came time for the World Series—the Yankees blew the Dodgers away, four games to one.

Bloody Feud Forces Tigers' Ty Cobb to Train With Reds

Detroit Tigers Hall of Famer Ty Cobb avoided a bloody feud with the New York Giants by finishing spring training with the Cincinnati Reds in 1917.

Even though the Georgia Peach was considered baseball's meanest and most ruthless brawler, he left his club for the safety of another team because he feared getting a serious injury that would keep him out of the lineup.

The Tigers and Giants were both training in Texas and agreed to play a series of exhibition games against each other throughout the area. New York was an aggressive, fighting team under the leadership of John McGraw. Detroit was a club with one star— Cobb.

The Giants started insulting Cobb even before their first exhibition game in Dallas. Both teams had checked into the same hotel, the Oriental, and when Cobb walked into the lobby, several Giants called him a "swell-head" and "show-off."

Cobb's blood boiled but he decided to keep cool and seek revenge later on the field, which he did. His first time up, Cobb singled. Then he yelled at New York second baseman Buck Herzog, "I'm coming down to get you!" Cobb took off on the first pitch, but catcher Lew McCarty, who had called for a pitchout, fired a perfect strike to Herzog that nailed Cobb by six feet.

Cobb came in with spikes high and sliced up Herzog in the thigh. As the two players hit the dirt, they started punching, wrestling, and clawing at each other, triggering a bench-clearing melee.

The umpires broke up the fray and tossed both men from the game.

TY COBB inflamed a bitter feud with a spikes-high slide.

That night, at the hotel, Herzog approached Cobb in the lobby and challenged him to finish the fight in Cobb's room.

"We'll each bring one man to back us up and [Tigers trainer]- Harry

Tuthill can referee," Herzog said.

"Okay, I'll see you at 9 o'clock," replied Cobb.

Herzog arrived with teammate Heinie Zimmerman to find Cobb already stripped at the waist—with a half dozen Detroit players in the room. Herzog didn't care. He wanted his piece of Cobb. The fight between the two men was violent but short as Cobb handily pummeled Herzog.

The next day, the two clubs traveled to Wichita Falls, Texas, where the brawl had made the papers. A huge crowd showed up for the game, hoping to see more fisticuffs. Everyone knew that the Giants would attempt to get even with Cobb at the first opportunity.

Cobb knew it, too, and chose not to play. He wasn't about to get beaned, spiked, or beat up during this or any other exhibition game with the Giants. It wasn't worth risking an injury that could affect his performance during the regular season.

So Cobb left his own team and finished the rest of spring training with the Cincinnati Reds. Tigers manager Hughie Jennings agreed with Cobb's decision, claiming that the star "was too valuable a piece of property to be brawling around with men that have less to risk."

While Cobb worked out peacefully with the Reds, the Giants and Tigers continued their rancorous tour which was lowlighted by more fights, beanballs, and bat-throwing.

When the exhibition season ended, McGraw and the entire Giants team stuck it to Cobb one more time. They sent him a wire that read: "It's safe to rejoin your club now. We've left." ◇

Spring Training for Major League Mascots

Baseball players aren't the only ones who head south to prepare for the season. For the first time, seven of major league baseball's team mascots joined players in Florida for their very own preseason tuneup. Andy Burstine (back to camera), from New York University, is shown leading the mascots through jumping jacks at the Philadelphia Phillies', spring training camp in Clearwater on March 5, 1991.

6-Day War of Words...

Longest Rain Delay Ever in Series Triggers Bitter Giants-A's Feud!

A monster rainstorm interrupted the 1911 World Series for nearly a week—and precipitated a bitter feud between the American and National Leagues that nearly washed the good will between them right down the drain.

The heavens opened up right after Game 3 of the Series between the New York Giants and Philadelphia Athletics and it rained for six days and six nights.

On the first day of rain, reporters covering the baseball drama were so bored they started writing about an almost-forgotten incident in Game 3 when Giants second baseman Buck Herzog spiked A's star Home Run Baker.

The next day, screaming headlines accused the Giants of playing "dirty ball." That sparked a series of charges and countercharges between New York manager John McGraw and A's skipper Connie Mack over the next two days.

Then American League President Ban Johnson leaped into the fray, calling the Giants a bunch of hoodlums and rowdies.

National League President Thomas Lynch responded in equally sharp tones, telling Johnson to go soak his head. Soon the newspapers were packed with wild stories about an impending war between the leagues.

On the sixth day of rain, Charles Ebbets, owner of the Brooklyn Dodgers, appealed for an armistice. "Let us be reasonable," he pleaded. "This feud will not only end the World Series but ruin the game permanently."

The teams and league officials agreed and decided to concentrate on baseball. The rain, which began falling heavily on the evening of October 17, finally ended on the morning of the

Yellow Baseballs Used in Major League Game

On August 2, 1938, the St. Louis Cardinals and Brooklyn Dodgers actually played a game with yellow baseballs.

It was an experiment to see if yellow baseballs were easier than white balls for batters to see and, thus, hit.

The yellow balls were introduced in the first game of a daytime doubleheader at Ebbets Field. The Dodgers won the game 6-2 with the Cardinals' Johnny Mize hitting the only home run. Reaction among the players was about exciting as an intentional walk. The batters generally were unimpressed with the yellow balls.

Conventional white balls were used in the second game. If the score was any indication, the batters found the white balls easier to follow. The Dodgers won the nightcap 9-3, and yellow balls went the way of flannel uniforms—into oblivion.

seventh day, October 24. Groundskeepers in Philadelphia poured gasoline on the water-logged field and burned it to help dry it out before Game 4 was played.

The A's won the soggy Series four games to two, without further feuding from either side. The big losers were the trouble-making reporters who fomented the needless rancor for the sake of selling newspapers. Many scribes frittered away their expense money in nightly poker games and ended up flat-busted. ◇

Backing Into the Record Book

When Jimmy Piersall of the New York Mets stroked his 100th career home run in 1963, he celebrated by running the bases backward.

James J. Corbett, First Baseman...

Boxing Champ Moonlights as Pro Ballplayer

Heavyweight boxing champion "Gentleman Jim" Corbett traded his fame in the ring for money on the diamond.

Corbett played professional baseball during and after his reign as champion—and was paid as much as half of the ball park gate.

In 1892, Gentleman Jim knocked out the favored John L. Sullivan—who held the world's heavyweight title for ten years—in 21 rounds and became a national celebrity.

Corbett's manager, Billy Brady, was a shrewd promoter who lined up all kinds of money-making appearances for Jim outside the ring. One of the most lucrative was on the baseball diamond. The popular boxer played first base in several exhibitions and in at least 28 official games in six minor leagues.

Gentleman Jim appeared in his first regulation game on Aug. 12, 1895, when he joined his younger brother Joe on the Scranton club of the Eastern League. The champ banged out two hits and drove in two runs. A month later, Corbett played for Toronto but went hitless in four trips to the plate.

Gentleman Jim had such star power that even after he was dethroned as the heavyweight champion in 1897 by Bob Fitzsimmons, fans still adored him. When Fitzsimmons, who knocked out Gentleman Jim in the 14th round, refused to give him a rematch, Corbett turned his attention back to baseball—and the fans flocked to see him.

Brady arranged for Corbett to play with minor league clubs for as much as half the gate. Between June 16 and Sept. 20, 1897, Gentleman Jim played in 26 regulation games.

He wore his own distinctive uniform—gray with black stockings and a checkered cap. And he drew very well. In Meriden, Connecticut, for example, 2,400 fans crowded the stands and another 1,000 stood on the ground to see him. Corbett scored two runs, banged out a hit, and handled 15 chances flawlessly at first base.

He made from $300 to $500 a game and is believed to have earned $17,000 in that one summer of playing minor league ball—a fortune in those days.

The presence of such a famous fighter led to some bizarre incidents. In Philadelphia, Corbett was slated to play in the second game of a doubleheader. When the first game was still tied 6-6 at the end of the 11th inning, they simply called the game. Since the restless crowd had come to see Corbett, the club owner said the heck with the opener and decided to start the nightcap. The boxer went hitless in a 1-1 game that was called by darkness after 11 innings.

When fights broke out in the stands or on the field, the fans would chant for Corbett to go into action, but Gentleman Jim stayed cool and out of any trouble.

Corbett's presence caused some other strange scenes. At Hartford, a boy in the dugout killed several mosquitoes on Corbett's back and sold them for a nickel each. Reading, a team known for arguing and bench jockeying, kept uncommonly quiet whenever it played against the former champ.

In his 26 official games at first base in

1897, Gentleman Jim batted .262, scored 13 runs, and knocked in 12. He smacked only two extra base hits in 103 at-bats, a double and a triple. He made 260 putouts, 10 assists, and 17 errors for a .943 fielding average.

Although the press and fans held his baseball playing in high regard, not everyone was impressed. After Corbett went hitless and committed two errors in a game, *The Youngstown Vindicator* said, "It was a big throng and an anxious crowd and they left the grounds in a disgusted mood because the game was lost and Corbett could not play marbles." ◇

Jackie Robinson Was *Not* Majors' First Black Player!

In 1884—63 years before Jackie Robinson broke the color barrier in the bigs—Moses Fleet Walker became the major league's first black player.

He played for the Toledo Mudhens of the American Association, which was considered a major league in those days.

Blacks were not that rare in organized baseball back then. At least 20 other black players were in the minor leagues prior to 1887. But then an unwritten code by Jim Crow advocates barred blacks from major league baseball—an unconscionable racist wall that wasn't torn down until the Brooklyn Dodgers put Jackie Robinson in the lineup in 1947.

But long before Robinson blazed a trail for blacks, Fleet Walker was leading the way. A barehanded catcher who lasted only a year in the majors, Walker played in 42 games for Toledo and batted .263.

After his baseball days, Walker edited a newspaper, operated a theatre, and patented several inventions in the motion picture industry. He died in 1924 at the age of 67.

His grave in Steubenville, Ohio, carries a marker placed by the John Heisman Club that reads: "The gentlemen was the first black major league player in the United States."◇

★★★

Rhubarb Rages Nearly Two Hours!

The Japanese hold the record for the longest known rhubarb in baseball history.

It raged for one hour and 52 minutes!

On Sept. 7, 1961, at Korakuen Stadium in Tokyo, the Yomiuri Giants and the Kokutetsu Swallows were tied 2-2 in the 11th inning when a Swallows runner was caught in a run-down between third and home and tagged out.

But the Swallows' manager insisted that the runner should be ruled safe because the Giants' third baseman had interfered with him. The umpires agreed, triggering a fire-storm of protest from the Giants.

Players, managers, and umpires ranted and raved in a screamfest that went on . . . and on . . . and on. The umps finally allowed the runner to score, giving the Swallows a 3-2 win.

Cleveland Indians Named After a Real-Life Indian

...But Booze Wrecked His Career

The Cleveland Indians are named after Louis Sockalexis, the first full-blooded American Indian to play in the majors. He was a dazzling outfielder with an incredible arm and a potent bat.

But he was also a tragic figure who blew his short-lived career because of booze.

Sockalexis, a Penobscot Indian whose grandfather had been a tribal chief, grew up in Maine where he was a tremendous high school athlete. In 1894, he played baseball for Holy Cross where in two seasons he batted an incredible .444. But all the while, he was battling the bottle.

He was reprimanded by the Jesuit fathers at Holy Cross for imbibing. Eventually, Sockalexis transferred to Notre Dame, but he didn't last long there. He was dismissed from the school after having been arrested for public drunkenness.

In 1897, Sockalexis tried out for the Cleveland Spiders (then in the National League) and was signed on the spot for $1,500. He was an instant success.

For the first two and a half months of the season, he became the hottest gate attraction in baseball, winning games with his hitting and saving games with his fielding. Somehow, he had managed to keep his drinking problem under control. By July 3, after 58 games, Sockalexis was hitting .328, with 40 runs scored, 39 RBI, and 16 stolen bases.

But then his career went into the dumpster—after a wild night in a whore house.

According to Spiders manager Patsy

LOUIS SOCKALEXIS let his thirst for booze ruin a great future.

Tebeau, Sockalexis had "celebrated the Fourth of July by an all-night carousal in a red light joint." The player got drunk, and, to elude the establishment's bouncer, leaped out of a second-floor window. Sockalexis injured his foot so badly that he played in only eight more games the rest of the year.

In one of the games, an 8-2 loss to Boston, *The Cleveland Plain Dealer* reported that Sockalexis "acted as if [he] had disposed of too many mint juleps previous to the game . . . Sockalexis . . . was directly responsible for all but one of Boston's runs . . . A lame foot is the Indian's excuse, but a Turkish bath and a good rest might be an excellent remedy."

Once his foot injury kept him out of the starting lineup, Sockalexis hit the bottle harder than ever before. In August, Sockalexis was fined and suspended by the club "for drinking a good deal."

The following year, Sockalexis played in only 21 games and hit .224. He played in just seven games the next season before he was released. He bounced around the New England minor league clubs . . . and then his life really hit the skids.

In 1900, he was charged with vagrancy and sentenced to 30 days in jail. "Sockalexis presented a sorry appearance," reported the *Holyoke* (Mass.) *Times*. "His clothing indicated that it had been worn for weeks without change. His hair was unkept, his face gaunt and bristly with several weeks' growth of beard, and his shoes so badly broken that his toes were protruding . . . He said, 'They liked me on the baseball field, and I liked firewater.' "

Sockalexis died in 1913 at the age of 42 while working as a wood cutter on a logging operation in Burlington, Maine.

Amazingly, this sick, tragic alcoholic became the inspiration for a revered children's book series and the name for an American League baseball team.

Frank Merriwell—the fictional sports hero who thrilled children for decades—is based on Sockalexis. Author Gilbert Patten, who was the manager of a Maine summer league, was so impressed by Sockalexis' performance on the diamond before joining Cleveland that he used him as the model for his popular Merriwell stories for boys, written under the pen name of Burt L. Standish.

In 1915, a Cleveland newspaper ran a contest to name the city's new American League team. A fan suggested the name Indians in honor of Louis Sockalexis. By then, a tale had spread that Sockalexis would have been a Hall of Famer if he hadn't suffered that foot injury when he heroically saved a baby in a runaway carriage. Club officials thought it was a great name.

And so the team became the Cleveland Indians. ◇

★★★

The Washington Padres?

In one of the most infamous goofs in baseball trading card history, Topps made cards for the *Washington* Padres.

Before the 1974 season when there was talk that the San Diego Padres would move to the nation's capital, Topps amended all the team's cards to read "Washington, Nat'l League" and put them on the market. But the Padres stayed put. Today, those cards are worth from $4 to $25 each.

Skunk Raises Stink in Pirates-Padres Game!

Horrified players froze in their tracks when a (gasp!) skunk coolly sauntered out onto the field, and, for seven long minutes, held up a 1986 game between the Pittsburgh Pirates and San Diego Padres.

The game, played at San Diego's Jack Murphy Stadium, was in the seventh inning when the black and white varmint crawled out from under a rolled-up tarpaulin along the right field wall and waltzed right up to the Padres' Steve Garvey at first base.

"I thought, 'What should I do?' " Garvey recalled. "Then I thought, 'I'm not going to do anything.' I didn't want to be sprayed with 'eau de skunk.' "

Umpire Dave Pallone suspended play while the walking stink bomb lazily wandered around the back of the infield checking things out. Players barely dared to breathe as the skunk ambled past them.

After seven minutes of sightseeing, the critter slipped under a tarp along the left field wall—and a sigh of relief went up from the two teams.

Said Garvey, "I've seen streakers, dogs, and cats . . . but it was the first time I've ever been skunk-delayed."

Forty-five years earlier, a wayward rabbit caused a hair-raising disturbance on the field during a 1941 exhibition game between the St. Louis Browns and a local team in Youngstown, Ohio.

Play was halted while the players, umpires, and bat boys tried to get the pesky little guy from underfoot. The shouting mob chased the rabbit back and forth from infield to outfield while the crowd roared with laughter. Finally, the harried hare hopped high into the grandstand—where a fan snatched him in midair with a one-handed grab.

After a six-minute delay, play resumed. Nobody knows the bunny's fate. One thing was certain, though. The rabbit gave the fans a hopping good time. ◇

First Baseman Travels First Class

In a wacky promotional stunt staged by Kansas City Athletics owner Charlie Finley, first baseman Ken Harrelson emerges from a chauffeur-driven limousine to deliver the starting lineup before a 1965 game.

PHOTO CREDITS